SWEET

LEVI ROOTS

MITCHELL BEAZLEY

First published in Great Britain in 2012 by Mitchell Beazley,
an imprint of Octopus Publishing Group Limited,
Endeavour House, 189 Shaftesbury Avenue, London WC2H 8JY.
www.octopusbooks.co.uk

An Hachette UK Company
www.hachette.co.uk

ISBN: 978 1 84533 665 3

A CIP record for this book is available from the British Library.

Printed and bound in China.

Consultants ~ Hattie Ellis and Diana Henry
Commissioning Editor ~ Becca Spry
Art direction, styling and design ~ Pene Parker
Illustration ~ Pene Parker
Head of Editorial ~ Tracey Smith
Senior Editor ~ Leanne Bryan
Senior Production Controller ~ Lucy Carter
Photographer ~ Chris Terry
Home Economist ~ Sara Lewis
Copy-editor ~ Emma Bastow
Proofreader ~ Salima Hirani
Indexer ~ Helen Snaith

Note ~ Where eggs are used in the recipes in this book they are always
large, unless otherwise specified.

LEVI ROOTS

SWEET

CONTENTS

INTRODUCTION

What does the word "sweet" conjure in your mind?
Sitting at home, relaxing in front of a DVD with a bowl
of sweet popcorn? Enjoying a homemade brownie?
Celebrating a birthday with a big, bountiful cake?
Whatever it is, I bet it's something good!

To me, "sweet" is about celebrating and sharing – and that's a beautiful thing! The fact that this book is called *Sweet* has more to do with attitude than sugar levels. Choosing to get together with family and friends and enjoy a particular moment by sharing a mouth-watering treat is part of the sweetness of life. You just have to listen to reggae music to know how important the sweet stuff is in the Caribbean. Bob Marley's "Guava Jelly" is just one of many songs that show how sweet flavours are associated with good times, pick-me-ups, aphrodisiacs, bonding and gifts. In Jamaica, there's a party vibe about sweet food.

And because we have a lot of parties in the Caribbean, we have discovered loads of ways to enjoy sweet flavours, and have made putting them together a subtle art. In this book, I explore the typical flavours of the Caribbean and how they marry with those recipes and ingredients that we know and love in the UK. I'm introducing my Sunshine Kit of flavours (ginger, allspice, nutmeg, Scotch Bonnet chillies, coriander, thyme and bay leaves) to familiar dishes such as crumbles and tarts, and serving up some typical Jamaican food as well.

How sweet it is...

There are ten chapters in this book, each offering many kinds of sweet foods for you to enjoy. The first chapter is full of cakes. The cake is the ultimate sharing-out sweet food, from which you cut slices for everyone, and there's something for everyone in this chapter, from extravagantly chocolately and indulgently fruity to temptingly spicy.

The next chapter covers biscuits and bars. Biscuits were the basis of my very first business. Back in the day, when I was still at secondary school, I was always coming up with ways to make money and I worked out that I could buy a packet of biscuits, sell them individually and double my capital.

It's a shame I didn't think to bake them myself, or I could have made a killing! I sold biscuits until I left school at 16. I love them and never have a cup of tea without one to hand, ready for dunking. If you're a biscuit fan like me, you'll find a good selection to choose from in this chapter.

Chapter three is all about pies and tarts. Who doesn't love pastries? In Jamaica, we bake in pots. You have a big pot full of boiling water, with a smaller pot inside for the dish – it's a bit like steaming a pudding. We have a saying that a good hot dish in the oven is 'hell a-top, hell a-bottom and "hallelujah" in the middle'! Check out my Jamaican takes on Bakewell Tart (*see* page 72) and Pecan Pie (*see* page 75).

The Fording, Cave River, Clarendon.

www.redstripe.net

Red Stripe

JAMAICA LAGER BEER

When I was growing up in the Caribbean, you'd get cream in only for very special occasions, to eat with a celebration cake or a comforting crumble. If the cream was in, you could expect a nice evening, because someone was really pushing the boat out with the sweet stuff. The recipes in the Creamy Puds chapter are all a bit special – perfect for when you really want to give the loved ones in your life an extravagant treat.

If you're into your comforting puddings, go straight to chapter five, which showcases my favourite baked and steamed puddings. Again, there's something for everyone here, and I've put a Caribbean twist on a few old favourites.

The next chapter is dedicated to fresh and fruity puddings. The Jamaican palate is seriously tuned into the fruit-sweet – this is the real fun sweet. When I was a boy, we never had toys or games for Christmas or birthday presents. It was always fruits we were given. There are fruit stalls everywhere in the Caribbean, dripping with fresh, ripe offerings. Then there's the fruit off the tree – it seems as if every second tree in Jamaica is a fruit tree. You eat lots of oranges because they fall off your trees into your garden.

(When I was a kid, you were told if you could remove the peel in one piece with a knife, you'd get a new shirt, which shows how good Jamaicans are at putting a fun twist on something simple, teaching kids to be careful with the knife and enjoy the orange afterwards.) The grapefruit, with its zingy flavour, is up there with the orange in Jamaica... and then, of course, there's the big, fancy mango. We used to give them to each other from our own trees. The type of mango you received was always revealing – if your friend gave you an East Indian mango, you'd know they thought a lot of you, because nobody gives those away easily!

We didn't have small berries in the Caribbean, but I love them. Strawberry fields forever! In the UK, we associate juicy berries with summer, fun times in the sun, watching sporting events such as Wimbledon or a cricket match with a bowl of delicious strawberries and cream in hand.

We love a good barbecue in Jamaica, and it's not just jerk chicken on the Caribbean flames – fruit also goes on the barbecue. Chapter seven contains some superlicious barbecued fruit recipes that will brighten up your summer, be it in your back garden, on a camping trip, in a city park or on the beach. A tropical fruit that's a favourite for this treatment is the pineapple. There are dozens of varieties of this wonderful fruit, and you can eat it, drink it and roast it. In the Caribbean, the pineapple symbolizes hospitality, so it's the ideal fruit to roll out when friends come over for a barbecue on a summer's afternoon. Pineapples and other fruits feature in this barbecue chapter because, in Jamaica, we often like to eat fruit charred and juicy for dessert.

Next comes a chapter that's nice and icy. Everyone likes ice cream or an ice lolly. In Jamaica, it's a welcome chiller in the summer heat, and the Fudge Man, who sells ice cream and sweeties, drives around on a moped with a little refrigerator from which many a cooling treat is dispensed. The old-fashioned horn that heralds his arrival is still the same today as it was in my childhood, while in Brixton, where I live, the ice cream van plays hip-hop! Mr Fudge also sells delicious sweets, and chapter nine provides recipes for a good selection of my favourite sweets – including fudge, of course, and plenty of chocolate treats.

Last but not least comes a chapter on drinks. Smoothies were created in Jamaica. When the blender came to town, rastas started mixing it up, fruit-wise. You chuck whatever you can into the blender, so long as it's fresh and wholesome and, on top of that, you add some oats and nuts to give the drink some body. In this chapter, you'll find a variety of drinks suitable for many occasions.

Home sweet home

More than anything, I want to celebrate Caribbean flavours in this book. There are many flavours that are distinctly Caribbean. For instance, where would the Caribbean be without rum? It's the staple liquor, made from the sugar that grows abundantly on the land. Rum can go into everything – sauces, smoothies, soups – there's always space for a bit of rum. Some are more refined than others, and the bad boy is white rum, one of the region's most successful exports. No one returns from Jamaica without a bottle to give as a present or share with family and friends. Rum is part of Jamaica's heritage. Many of the older generation worked in sugar cane or rum, and there are plantations and rum factories everywhere. You use rum as a liquor, in the kitchen, when you have a cold (my grandparents would rub it on my head) and it's even used in church to anoint people. We respect and enjoy this important commodity greatly.

There are many sources of sweetness in the Caribbean that I explore in the recipes in this book. As already mentioned, fruit-sweet is a big Caribbean taste. Where there's fruit, there are flowers, and where there are flowers, there are bees. Honey is another key ingredient. I grew up enjoying the honey produced by my grandfather's bees. I did get stung – as my grandfather said, if you trouble the bees, they trouble you back. But this didn't put me off and we ate the honeycomb using a piece of banana leaf as a plate. My grandfather showed me how to take the comb from the hive. Comb honey is the most wonderful thing ever. Its flavour depends on what the bees have been feeding on. In Jamaica, honey is seen as a blessed food, the food of the Gods, ambrosia that's added to many sweet dishes.

Of course the main source of sweetness is from sugar. I never saw white sugar when I was growing up – we always had brown sugar, which has more flavour. That's why I still use plenty of it in my cooking, whether its Demerara sugar or light and dark muscovado sugars. Sweet milk, or condensed milk, originally arrived in Jamica by boat, and is also used a good deal in Caribbean cooking.

Caribbean cooking dances with spices, and many of them are used in both sweet and savoury dishes. Pimento, or allspice, is used in cakes and puddings as well as in porridges, soups and jerk flavourings on the barbeque. Nutmeg and vanilla are ubiquitous. Vanilla is a hugely popular flavour that is used widely in the Caribbean. We also like a bit of heat in sweet food, and Scotch Bonnet chilli pepper is often found in chocolate and sweet foods. You'll find it creeping into a few recipes in this book, too.

Sweet memories

So here's a book for you to take into the kitchen and have some fun with. It's written for children as well as adults, because kids love sweet things and it's great to get them to participate in cooking their favourite sweet recipes. Making sweet dishes with your kids is one way of getting them into the kitchen to learn what's gone into a dish and to respect food. And it's very Caribbean for everybody to get involved in making a meal. The adults might prepare the fish or meat while the young ones make the coconut drops or peel the mangoes. Food brings people together and gives them a reason to want to come round and visit each other, and sweet food, in particular, is about that gathering and sharing of the family vibe.

Sweet foods are often the last taste of a meal that you take away with you along with your memories of a happy time. I'm hoping that this book will help you to make lots of good memories, so here's to you enjoying yourself, treating your family and friends and to all the bountiful sweet times to come!

Levi Roots

Gᵈᵉ FABRIQUE
DE
BOISSONS GAZEUSES
& SIROPS

MAISON FONDÉE en 1818

MARQUE DÉPOSÉE

SIROP
PUR SUCRE

MOTTE-TOURTEL
11, AVENUE ROGER SALENGRO (EX ARENC)
TEL.NA 04-16 MARSEILLE TEL.NA 04-16

FABRIQUE DE SIROPS

SIROP
PUR SUCRE
LOUIS BOYER
CAMARET
(VAUCLUSE)

MABEREH DOUIN & JOUNEAU PARIS

SUGAR, Z.

WILLS'S CIGARETTES.

SUGAR - CASTER.

Mazzoni Cristina Serie 2003

PLAYER'S CIGARETTES

SUGAR, 1.

PLAYER'S

SUGAR, 3.

Fowlers
WEST INDIA
TREACLE
AND
PURE CANE GOLDEN SYRUP

FOWLER'S
WEST INDIA
TREACLE

RECIPES FOR THE HOME

FABRIQUE

CRÈME
FAM
LOU
C

MANGO & PASSION FRUIT CAKE

A fabulocious cake! Light, moist, and with one of my favourite fillings. This is great for a special celebration, especially in winter and spring when exotic fruits are around but summer fruits are a long way off.

Serves 8

350g (12oz) unsalted butter, slightly softened, plus extra for greasing

350g (12oz) caster sugar

finely grated rind of 3 unwaxed oranges

6 free-range eggs, lightly beaten

350g (12oz) self-raising flour, sifted

2 tbsp orange juice

For the filling:

2 ripe passion fruit

1 small ripe mango

juice and finely grated rind of 1 unwaxed orange

juice and finely grated rind of 2 unwaxed limes

120g (4¼oz) granulated sugar

175ml (6fl oz) whipping cream

icing sugar to taste, plus extra for dusting

1. Preheat the oven to 200°C/fan 180°C/gas mark 6. Beat the butter and sugar together, using an electric mixer or by hand, until pale and fluffy. Add the orange rind and beat again. Add the eggs one at a time, beating well after each addition. (If the mixture starts to curdle add a tablespoon of the flour and beat well.)

2. Using a large metal spoon, fold in the flour. Add the orange juice and mix gently to combine. Pour into 2 greased and base-lined 20cm (8in) diameter round cake tins and bake for 35—40 minutes, or until a skewer inserted into the centre comes out clean. Turn out onto a wire rack and leave to cool.

3. To make the filling, halve the passion fruit and scoop out the pulp and seeds. Peel, stone and roughly chop the mango. Place both fruits in a small saucepan set over a medium heat. Add the orange and lime juice and rinds. Add the sugar and bring to the boil. Cook for 8 minutes, stirring, until the mixture is thick and jam-like. Remove the pan from the heat and leave the mixture to cool.

4. Whip the cream into medium peaks and add icing sugar to taste. Place one of the cakes onto a serving plate. Spread the cream over the cake and spoon over the fruit filling. Place the other cake on top and dust with icing sugar.

PASSION FRUIT & RASPBERRY ROULADE

This gorgeous summer dessert can be made with blueberries instead of raspberries, if you prefer. The only tricky bit is rolling up your sponge into a Swiss roll shape – have help standing by in case you need it. You'll feel so pleased when you've put it all together!

Serves 8

6 free-range eggs, separated

100g (3½oz) caster sugar, plus extra for dusting

finely grated rind of 2 unwaxed lemons and juice of 1

4 tbsp plain flour, sifted

unsalted butter, for greasing

caster sugar, for sprinkling

7 large, really ripe passion fruit

200ml (⅓ pint) double cream

icing sugar, to taste

200–275g (7–9¾oz) lemon curd

200g (7oz) raspberries

1. Preheat the oven to 220°C/fan 200°C/gas mark 7. Beat the egg yolks and sugar together, using an electric mixer or by hand, until pale and fluffy. Add the lemon juice and rind and beat again.

2. In a separate bowl, whisk the egg whites until soft peaks form. Using a large metal spoon, add a spoonful of the egg whites to the yolk mixture and gently fold in, then fold in the rest. Carefully fold in the flour. Pour into a greased and base-lined 30 × 35cm (12 × 14in) shallow rectangular tin and bake for 10 minutes until pale golden and just set in the middle. Leave to cool in the tin for a couple of minutes before turning out onto a large rectangle of nonstick baking paper lightly sprinkled with caster sugar. Carefully peel away the paper used to line the tin and leave to cool.

3. Halve the passion fruit and scoop out the pulp and seeds. Whip the cream into medium peaks and add enough icing sugar to satisfy your sweet tooth. Spread the lemon curd over the cake, then spread the cream over the top. Spoon over the passion fruit and raspberries. Roll the roulade into a Swiss-roll shape, using the baking paper to help hold it together. It may crack a little, but don't panic. Transfer to a serving plate (this is where you might need an extra pair of hands) and sprinkle with a little caster sugar.

HONEY & TAMARIND CAKE WITH LIME ICING

Bees are my friends in the garden, producing delicious honey. Here, the fruit of their labour is combined with the mighty tamarind pod to make a cake that's nice and spicy.

Serves 6–8

100g (3½oz) unsalted butter, plus extra for greasing

100g (3½oz) dark brown muscovado sugar

100g (3½oz) clear honey

175g (6oz) self-raising flour

5 cardamom pods

large pinch of salt

½ tsp ground cinnamon

½ tsp finely grated nutmeg

1 tsp ground ginger

2 tbsp tamarind paste

2 free-range eggs, lightly beaten

For the lime icing:

175g (6oz) icing sugar

1½ tbsp lime juice

black and yellow icing pens, to draw a bee on top (optional)

1. Preheat the oven to 200°C/fan 180°C/gas mark 6. Place the butter, sugar and honey in a saucepan set over a low heat and heat until the butter and sugar have melted, stirring occasionally. Remove the pan from the heat and leave to cool.

2. Meanwhile, sift the flour into a mixing bowl. Crush the cardamom pods and discard the husks, then finely grind the seeds using a pestle and mortar or whizz in a small food processor. Add to the flour along with the salt and remaining spices. Stir to mix well.

3. Add the butter mixture, tamarind paste and eggs to the flour mixture. Stir until well combined, then pour into a greased and base-lined 1 litre (1¾ pint) loaf tin. Bake for 40 minutes, or until a skewer inserted into the centre of the cake comes out clean. Leave to cool in the tin for 10 minutes, then turn out onto a wire rack to cool completely.

4. For the lime icing, mix together the icing sugar and lime juice until smooth and glossy. Place the cake onto a serving plate and spread the icing over the top. Leave to set. If you like, you can then use black and yellow icing pens to draw a big bee on top, with plenty of zeds for the buzzzzzzzzzzz!

ALMOND CAKE WITH LIME & CARDAMOM SYRUP

This is my favourite kind of cake as you don't need any kitchen gadgets to make it, just a simple wooden spoon. It's based on the cakes that are popular in Greece and Turkey, which are made using oil and yogurt. This recipe produces a lovely moist cake.

Serves 8–10

250g (9oz) ground almonds
100g (3½oz) self-raising flour
150g (5½oz) caster sugar
1½ tsp baking powder
pinch of salt
160ml (5½fl oz) sunflower oil, plus extra for greasing
2 free-range eggs, lightly beaten
250g (9oz) Greek yogurt, plus extra to serve
finely grated rind of 4 unwaxed limes
icing sugar, for dusting

For the lime and cardamom syrup:
10 cardamom pods
300ml (½ pint) water
225g (8oz) granulated sugar
juice of 8 limes

1. Preheat the oven to 200°C/fan 180°C/gas mark 6. Place the ground almonds, flour, caster sugar, baking powder and salt in a large bowl and mix. Make a well in the centre.

2. In a separate bowl, combine the oil, eggs, yogurt and lime rind, then pour into the well in the flour mixture. Beat together using a wooden spoon until smooth, gradually drawing in all of the dry ingredients. Pour into a greased and base-lined 20cm (8in) diameter round loose-bottomed cake tin and bake in the centre of the oven for 40 minutes, or until a skewer inserted into the centre of the cake comes out clean. Leave to cool on a wire rack.

3. Meanwhile, make the lime and cardamom syrup. Crush the cardamom pods and place in a small saucepan set over a medium heat. Add the remaining syrup ingredients and bring to the boil, stirring gently. Boil until reduced by half and slightly syrupy. Strain and discard the cardamom pods seeds and husks.

4. Run a knife around the inside of the cake tin, but don't remove it. Pierce the cake all over with a skewer and pour the syrup on top. Leave for a few hours, or overnight, to allow the cake to soak up the syrup. Remove the cake from the tin, peel the baking paper from its base and place it on a serving plate. Dust with icing sugar and serve with Greek yogurt.

TROPICAL FRUIT CAKE

This cake is my take on a traditional fruit cake and makes a delicious summery alternative to the darker type you get at Christmas. You can buy tropical dried-fruit in the baking section of most supermarkets, or make your own by mixing together dried mango, pineapple, papaya and currants.

Serves 16–20

300g (10½oz) dried tropical fruit, roughly chopped

200ml (⅓ pint) dark rum

2 tbsp rosewater or orange-blossom water

100g (3½oz) pecans, roughly chopped, plus 50g (1¾oz) whole pecans

4 pieces of preserved stem ginger in syrup, finely chopped

finely grated rind of 1 unwaxed orange

300g (10½oz) unsalted butter, softened, plus extra for greasing

100g (3½oz) light muscovado sugar

100g (3½oz) caster sugar

5 free-range eggs

300g (10½oz) plain flour

1. The night before making your cake, place the dried fruit in a bowl and pour over the rum and rosewater or orange-blossom water. Stir, cover and leave to stand overnight. When you are ready to make the cake, add the chopped pecans, stem ginger and orange rind and stir.

2. Preheat the oven to 180°C/fan 160°C/gas mark 4. Beat the butter and sugars together until pale and fluffy. Add the eggs one by one, alternating with spoonfuls of flour (reserving 75g/2¾oz), beating well after each addition.

3. Mix the reserved flour with the fruit mixture, stirring to coat well (coating the fruit with flour will help to prevent it from sinking to the bottom when the cake is baked), then stir the fruit into the batter. Pour the mixture into a greased and lined 26cm (10½in) diameter round loose-bottomed cake tin, making a dip in the centre with the back of a spoon to help the cake rise evenly. Cook on a baking sheet in the centre of the oven.

4. After 15 minutes, when the cake has set slightly, arrange the whole pecans on top, pushing them down slightly. Return the cake to the oven for a further 45 minutes.

5. Reduce the heat to 160°C/fan 140°C/gas mark 3 and bake for a further 1½ hours, or until a skewer inserted into the centre of the cake comes out clean. Leave to cool, then turn out the cake and wrap it in nonstick baking paper or foil. This cake keeps well in an airtight tin for up to a week.

CHOCOLATE & LIME CAKE

Chocolate and lime go so well together. However, you can make lemon icing, if you prefer, by replacing the lime with a large lemon.

Serves 8

175g (6oz) unsalted butter,
   softened, plus extra for greasing
175g (6oz) soft dark brown sugar
3 free-range eggs
135g (4¾oz) self-raising flour
4 tbsp cocoa powder
1 tbsp milk or rum, if necessary

For the candied lime rind:
50g (1¾oz) granulated sugar
4 tbsp water
grated rind of 3 unwaxed limes

For the buttercream:
100g (3½oz) unsalted butter,
   slightly softened
200g (7oz) icing sugar
grated rind of 3 unwaxed limes,
   and juice of 2–3 (depending
   on their size – you need
   enough juice to make a firm
   but spreadable buttercream)
dark chocolate, roughly
   chopped, to decorate

1. Preheat the oven to 200°C/fan 180°C/gas mark 6. Beat the butter and sugar together, using an electric mixer or by hand, until pale and fluffy. Add the eggs one at a time, beating between each addition. Fold in the flour and cocoa powder. If the mixture is very stiff, stir in a tablespoon of milk (or rum!) at this stage. Spoon into a greased and base-lined 20cm (8in) diameter, 2cm (¾in) deep round cake tin and bake for 35–40 minutes or until a skewer inserted into the centre of the cake comes out clean. Turn out the cake onto a wire rack and leave to cool.

2. Meanwhile, make the candied lime rind. Place the sugar and water in a small saucepan set over a low heat and stir until the sugar dissolves. Add the lime rind and cook over a medium heat for 7–10 minutes, stirring occasionally and reducing the heat as the syrup thickens, until the sugar syrup has reduced and the lime rind is soft (the syrup should look like marmalade). Using a fork, transfer the rind to a baking sheet lined with nonstick baking paper and leave to cool and harden.

3. To make the buttercream, beat the butter and icing sugar together, with an electric mixer (start off gently or the icing sugar will fly everywhere) or by hand, until pale and light, but don't beat it for so long that it gets too fluffy. Add the lime rind and juice and beat again. Chill in the refrigerator until the buttercream is firm but spreadable.

4. Spread the buttercream over the top of the cake using a palette knife. Decorate with candied lime rind and dark chocolate.

WHITE CHOCOLATE & VANILLA CAKE WITH ~~DARK~~ CHOCOLATE SWIRLS

milk

Serves 10–12

135g (4¾oz) unsalted butter, softened, plus extra for greasing

225g (8oz) caster sugar

175g (6oz) white chocolate, broken into pieces

250ml (9fl oz) milk

1½ tsp vanilla extract

4 free-range egg whites

300g (10½oz) self-raising flour, sifted

pinch of salt

100g (3½oz) dark chocolate, broken into pieces

For the white chocolate ganache:

225g (8oz) white chocolate, broken into pieces

200g (7oz) crème fraîche

½ tsp vanilla extract

lemon juice, to taste

A stunning-looking number! One for a very special occasion...

1. Preheat the oven to 200°C/fan 180°C/gas mark 6. Beat the butter and sugar together, using an electric mixer or by hand, until pale and fluffy. Melt the white chocolate in a bowl set over a saucepan of simmering water, ensuring that the base of the bowl doesn't touch the water. Set aside to cool a little.

2. Beat the milk, vanilla extract and egg whites together. Add to the creamed butter and sugar a little at a time, alternating with spoonfuls of the flour, and beat with the mixer on a low setting or stir gently by hand after each addition. Add the salt and melted white chocolate and beat to combine. Pour into a greased and base-lined 23cm (9in) diameter round cake tin and bake for 45 minutes, or until a skewer inserted into the centre of the cake comes out clean. Cool in the tin for 10 minutes, then turn out onto a cooling rack.

3. To make the white chocolate ganache, melt the chocolate in a bowl set over a saucepan of simmering water, as above. Add the crème fraîche and beat until the mixture is completely smooth. Add the vanilla extract and some lemon juice (this takes the edge off the sweetness, but don't add so much that you overwhelm the flavour of the vanilla). Set aside to firm up (or stick it in the refrigerator for a bit) then spread it over the top and sides of the cake. Leave to set.

4. Melt the dark chocolate in a bowl set over a saucepan of simmering water, as above. Using a metal spoon, scoop up the melted chocolate and drizzle it over the surface of the cake (or spoon it into a cone made from nonstick baking paper, snip the end off, then gently squeeze to release the chocolate and drizzle over the cake). Let the topping set before serving.

White Chocolate & Raspberry Sponge

Serves 8

- 175g (6oz) unsalted butter, softened, plus extra for greasing
- 175g (6oz) caster sugar
- 3 free-range eggs
- 175g (6oz) self-raising flour
- ½ tsp baking powder
- 1 tbsp milk, if necessary
- 170g–340g (½–1 × 340g jar) raspberry jam
- 200g (7oz) raspberries
- 10g (¼ oz) white chocolate, grated, to decorate

For the white-chocolate icing:
- 90g (3¼oz) white chocolate, broken into pieces
- 150g (5½oz) unsalted butter, softened
- 150g (5½oz) icing sugar
- 2 tbsp elderflower cordial

This cake is one of the best I've ever eaten. It looks great AND it's easy to make.

1. Preheat the oven to 200°C/fan 180°C/gas mark 6. Beat together the butter and sugar, using an electric mixer or by hand, until pale and fluffy. Add the eggs one at a time, alternating with spoonfuls of the flour and baking powder, beating well between each addition. Add the milk, if necessary, to achieve a dropping consistency.

2. Divide the mixture between 2 greased and base-lined 20cm (8in) diameter round loose-bottomed cake tins and bake for 20–25 minutes, until brown on top (this sponge is not a high-riser but is rich and buttery). Cool in the tins for a few minutes, then turn out onto a wire rack and leave to cool completely.

3. Meanwhile, make the white-chocolate icing. Melt the chocolate in a bowl set over a saucepan of simmering water, ensuring that the base of the bowl doesn't touch the water. Set aside to cool slightly. Beat the butter, then add the icing sugar a little at a time and beat until well incorporated. Beat in the white chocolate and elderflower cordial.

4. Place one cake on a serving plate. Spread over a third of the icing, then all the raspberry jam. Top with half the raspberries, positioned around the edges of the cake. Put the other cake on top, spread with the remainder of the icing and decorate with the rest of the raspberries and the grated white chocolate.

MINI MARMALADE MUFFINS WITH LIME GLAZE

A jar of lime marmalade gives these mini muffins a wonderful Caribbean flavour. They're lovely and moist, too. It's best to eat them on the day they are made; in fact, they're perfect in the afternoon with a strong coffee.

Makes 20

250g (9oz) plain flour

150g (5½oz) wholemeal flour

1 tbsp baking powder

100g (3½oz) soft light brown sugar

275ml (9½fl oz) milk

1 free-range egg

35g (1¼oz) unsalted butter, melted, plus extra for greasing

25g (1oz) pecans, roughly chopped

225g (8oz) lime marmalade

2 tbsp lime juice

finely grated rind of 2 unwaxed limes

For the lime glaze:

2–3 tbsp lime juice

250g (9oz) icing sugar

1. Preheat the oven to 200°C/fan 180°C/gas mark 6. Sift both flours and the baking powder into a large mixing bowl. Add the sugar and stir to combine, then make a well in the centre. Mix the milk, egg and melted butter together, then gradually pour the mixture into the centre of the dry ingredients, stirring to incorporate the dry ingredients (take care not to over-mix, as this can spoil the texture of the muffins). Add the pecans, marmalade and lime juice and rind and stir.

2. Divide the mixture between 20 cups of a greased mini-muffin tin (you can use paper cases, if you like) and bake for 20 minutes or until a skewer inserted into the centre of one of the muffins comes out clean. Allow the muffins to cool in the tin for 10 minutes, then run a knife between the muffins and the tin (unless you have used paper cases), turn out onto a wire rack and leave to cool.

3. While the muffins cool, make the lime glaze. Stir enough lime juice into the icing sugar to form a thick paste, then set aside to allow it to firm up a little,but not set. Once firm, spoon the glaze over the muffins, allowing it to run down their sides. Leave the icing to set, then serve.

BLOOD ORANGE CUPCAKES

Blood oranges are only in season for about six weeks after Christmas, and I just can't resist their fabulocious colour. If you can't get hold of whole blood oranges, use ready-squeezed blood orange juice. These cupcakes also taste great when made using juice from regular oranges.

Makes 24

250g (9oz) unsalted butter, softened
250g (9oz) caster sugar
250g (9oz) self-raising flour
4 free-range eggs
6 tbsp blood orange juice
finely grated rind of 2 unwaxed blood oranges (or regular oranges)
crystallized flowers or sugar flowers, to decorate

For the icing:
100g (3½oz) icing sugar
1½ tbsp blood orange juice

1. Preheat the oven to 220°C/fan 200°C/gas mark 7. Whizz the butter, sugar, flour, eggs, orange juice and rind together in a food processor, or using an electric mixer, until combined. (Or beat the butter and sugar together by hand, until pale and fluffy. Add the eggs one at a time, alternating with spoonfuls of the flour and beating well after each addition. Finally, stir in the orange juice and rind.)

2. Divide the mixture between paper cases set in 2 × 12-hole cupcake tins, filling each case about two-thirds full. Bake for 20 minutes or until golden and a skewer inserted into the centre of one of the cakes comes out clean. Leave to cool in the tin for a couple of minutes, then transfer to a wire rack to cool completely.

3. Meanwhile, make the icing. Sift the icing sugar into a bowl and add the orange juice. Stir to make a smooth icing, then place in the refrigerator for a few minutes to harden a little. Spread the icing over the cooled buns using a palette knife and leave to set a little.

4. Now decorate — I use crystallized flowers (violets look wild against the orange icing) but sugar flowers look great too. Serve once the icing has set completely.

29

Tropical Butterfly Cakes

Here's a great recipe for getting the kids involved in the kitchen. Jamaica is the land of butterflies as it is abundant with flowers, which invite butterflies and bees alike. You get them fluttering all over the place, in every colour – and some are almost as big as these little cakes!

Makes 10

125g (4½oz) unsalted butter, softened

85g (3oz) light muscovado sugar

50g (1¾oz) caster sugar

150g (5½oz) self-raising flour

1 tsp baking powder

2 free-range eggs

For the buttercream:

85g (3oz) unsalted butter, softened

100g (3½oz) icing sugar

2–3 tbsp maple syrup

To decorate:

Smarties

coloured sprinkles

1. Preheat the oven to 200°C/fan 180°C/gas mark 6. Beat the butter and both sugars together, using an electric mixer or by hand, until pale and fluffy. Add the eggs one at a time to the butter and sugar mixture, alternating with spoonfuls of the flour and baking powder, beating well after each addition. Divide the mixture between 10 foil or paper cake cases set in a cake tray.

2. Bake for 15 minutes, or until the cakes are brown and risen and a skewer inserted into the centre of one of them comes out clean. Leave to cool in the tin for 10 minutes, then transfer to a wire rack to cool completely.

3. Meanwhile, make the buttercream. Beat the butter and icing sugar together until smooth, then stir in maple syrup, to taste.

4. Using a small, sharp knife, cut a shallow circle from the top of each cake to leave a hollow, then cut each circle in half to make the butterfly wings. Spoon the buttercream into the hole on the top of each cake and place a set of wings on top. Decorate the cakes with sugar-coated chocolate beans and sprinkles to make them look like tropical butterflies.

LEVI'S LOVE BUNS

These pretty cakes are for the sweetheart in your life! Make the filling and assemble them just before you want to serve them, as the cream tastes much better when it's fresh.

Makes 10

125g (4½oz) unsalted butter, softened

125g (4½oz) caster sugar

2 free-range eggs, lightly beaten

70g (2½oz) self-raising flour

70g (2½oz) ground almonds

½ tsp baking powder

½ tsp vanilla extract

finely grated rind of 1 unwaxed lemon

2 tbsp milk

icing sugar, for dusting

For the topping:

150g (5½oz) mascarpone cheese

4 tbsp crème fraîche

3 tbsp icing sugar

squeeze of lemon juice

100g (3½oz) raspberries

1 tsp crème de framboise or crème de cassis

1. Preheat the oven to 220°C/fan 200°C/gas mark 7. Whizz the butter, sugar, eggs, flour, ground almonds, baking powder, vanilla extract and lemon rind together in a food processor, or using an electric mixer, until smooth. With the motor running, add the milk a little at a time until the mixture has a soft, dropping consistency. (Alternatively, beat the butter and sugar together by hand until pale and fluffy, then add the eggs one at a time, alternating spoonfuls of the flour, ground almonds and baking powder, and beating well after each addition. Stir in the vanilla extract and lemon rind, then add the milk a little at a time until the mixture has a soft, dropping consistency.)

2. Divide the mixture between 10 paper muffin cases set in a muffin tin and bake for 15—20 minutes, or until the buns are golden and a skewer inserted into the centre of one of them comes out clean. Leave to cool in the tin for a couple of minutes, then transfer to a wire rack to cool completely. Cut a shallow circle from the top of each bun to leave a hollow, then cut each circle into a heart shape and set aside.

3. To make the topping, beat the mascarpone, crème fraîche, icing sugar and lemon juice together until smooth. Carefully stir in 70g (2½oz) of the raspberries and the fruit liqueur. The raspberries will get slightly crushed and the mixture should be marbled pink in colour, but don't overmix it. Spoon the filling into the shallow hole on the top of each cake. Top with the remaining raspberries and the sponge hearts and dust lightly with icing sugar. Serve wrapped in cupcake wrappers.

CARDAMOM & ALLSPICE BROWNIES

The combination of cardamom and allspice in these brownies really sets them aside from regular chocolate brownies. Allspice is the classic spice of Jamaican cooking. We call it pimento, and it marries well with cardamom.

Makes 24

250g (9oz) dark chocolate

250g (9oz) unsalted butter, plus extra for greasing

5 free-range eggs

300g (10½oz) caster sugar

85g (3oz) light muscovado sugar

125g (4½oz) plain flour

2 tbsp cocoa powder

100g (3½oz) ground almonds

seeds from 6 cardamom pods, crushed

½ tsp ground allspice

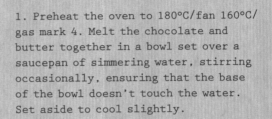

1. Preheat the oven to 180°C/fan 160°C/gas mark 4. Melt the chocolate and butter together in a bowl set over a saucepan of simmering water, stirring occasionally, ensuring that the base of the bowl doesn't touch the water. Set aside to cool slightly.

2. Beat the eggs and both sugars together, using an electric mixer or by hand, for 5 minutes or until thick and the whisk leaves a trail when lifted out of the mixture. Add the chocolate and butter mixture and beat again until combined. Fold in the flour, cocoa powder, ground almonds, cardamom seeds and allspice.

3. Pour the mixture into a greased and base-lined 33 × 23cm (13 × 9in), 4—5cm (1½—2in) deep rectangular roasting tin and bake for 30—35 minutes, or until firm but still leaving a slightly gooey trace on a knife that is inserted into the centre.

4. Leave to cool in the tin, then cut into squares before serving.

BISCUITS & BARS

Roumania. BUCAREST.
La Chambre des Députés.

COLLECTION DES CHOCOLATS SUCHARD

PLAYER'S CIGARETTES

COCOA, 1.

COCOA, 2.

BRAZIL

COFFEE ALLY GROWN.

FFEE BEANS.

KAKAO

Berg

200 ml
170 kcal
9% GDA*

%GDA* pro Glas
717 kJ/ 9%
pro Glas**

e schützen

hrliche Informationen
aktivleben.com

5a

ld Coast

Important Industries of the British Empire

THE GOLD COAST : COCOA

The Gold Coast is one of the most important sources of the world's cocoa supply, and in 1937 the Colony exported 236,000 tons. The cacao tree yields on an average 20 pods every year. These pods are gathered by means of long bamboo poles, cut open, and the beans extracted (as shown in the picture). The beans are then fermented and dried. It is estimated that one cacao tree gives an annual average yield of 2 lbs. of dried beans. (Imperial Institute Diorama.)

Typhoo Series of 25   No. 18

ica C. robusta

9 ♠

Supreme Blend

COFFEE

DE KOFFIE
2. — Hoofdsoorten en hun kweek
LIEBIG PRODUKTEN: heilzaam voor het organisme
Verklaring o

DE KOFFIE
1. — Historiek van de koffie als drank
OXO BOUILLON: rijk aan vleesextract
Nadruk verboden   Verklaring o

Tropical Florentines

Florentines are elegant little biscuits that go well with coffee or a bowl of ice cream.

Makes 12–14

50g (1¾oz) unsalted butter, cut into pieces

50g (1¾oz) light muscovado sugar

25g (1oz) clear honey

25g (1oz) plain flour

100g (3½oz) dried mango, chopped

100g (3½oz) pecans, chopped

100g (3½oz) dark chocolate, broken into pieces

1. Preheat the oven to 180°C/fan 160°C/gas mark 4. Melt the butter, sugar and honey together in a saucepan set over a low heat, stirring occasionally. Remove from the heat and stir in the flour, mango and pecans. Mix until smooth.

2. Drop dessertspoonfuls of the mixture, quite widely spaced, onto baking sheets lined with nonstick baking paper. Spread into thinnish rounds using the back of a spoon, leaving space for them to spread. Bake for 10–12 minutes, ensuring the biscuits do not burn. Cool on the baking sheet for 10 minutes, then use a palette knife to carefully transfer the biscuits to a wire rack. Leave to cool completely.

3. Meanwhile, melt the chocolate in a bowl set over a saucepan of simmering water, ensuring that the bottom of the bowl doesn't touch the water. When the florentines are cool, dip each one into the melted chocolate to half cover. Leave to set on a tray lined with nonstick baking paper (you can get them to set quickly by putting the biscuits in the refrigerator for 30 minutes).

BILLIONAIRE'S SHORTBREAD

Millionaire's shortbread has caramel on top and a dark-chocolate topping.
My billionaire's version has chocolate shortbread, for dedicated chocoholics.

Makes about 36

For the chocolate shortbread:
150g (5½oz) cold unsalted
   butter, cut into small pieces,
   plus extra for greasing
150g (5½oz) plain flour
60g (2¼oz) caster sugar
2 tbsp cocoa powder

For the caramel:
397g can condensed milk
150g (5½oz) unsalted butter
50g (1¾oz) light muscovado
   sugar
1 tsp vanilla extract

For the chocolate topping:
200g (7oz) dark chocolate
50g (1¾oz) milk chocolate
50g (1¾oz) white chocolate

1. Preheat the oven to 160°C/fan 140°C/gas
mark 3. Whizz all the shortbread ingredients
together in a food processor until the mixture
resembles fine breadcrumbs. (Alternatively,
put the butter and flour in a large bowl and rub
together with your fingertips, then stir in the
sugar and cocoa powder.) Press into a greased
and base-lined 20cm (8in) square baking tin.
Bake for 45—50 minutes, or until the shortbread
is firm and slightly coming away from the edges
of the tin. Leave to cool in the tin.

2. Meanwhile, put the caramel ingredients
in a saucepan set over a medium heat. Cook,
stirring continuously, for 3—5 minutes or
until you have a thick, fudgy mixture. Spread
over the shortbread and set aside to cool.

3. Melt the dark chocolate in a bowl set over
a saucepan of simmering water, ensuring that
the base of the bowl doesn't touch the water.
Pour over the caramel layer and spread across
the surface using a pallet knife. Leave to cool
for around 15 minutes.

4. Melt the milk chocolate in the same
way. Dip a metal spoon into the melted
milk chocolate and drizzle it over the
dark chocolate layer. (Alternatively, spoon
the melted chocolate into a cone made from
non-stick baking paper, snip off the end and
gently squeeze to release the chocolate.)
Chill the shortbread in the refrigerator
for 15—30 minutes then repeat with the white
chocolate. Chill again until firm enough to cut.

5. Cut into pieces measuring around 3cm (1¼in)
square and store in an airtight container for
up to 4 days.

THUMBPRINT COOKIES

These cookies are rich, buttery and very more-ish. You can replace the hazelnuts with walnuts, pecans or almonds, and use any kind of jam, but as the dough is so sweet, you should choose one with a little bite.

Makes 45

225g (8oz) unsalted butter, softened
70g (2½oz) icing sugar
1 tsp vanilla extract
150g (5½oz) plain flour
70g (2½oz) cornflour
70g (2½oz) hazelnuts

To finish:
1 × 340g jar of raspberry jam
icing sugar, for dusting

1. Beat the butter and icing sugar together, using an electric mixer or by hand, until pale and fluffy. Add the vanilla extract and beat the mixture some more.

2. Add both flours and the hazelnuts, a little at a time, stirring well between each addition. Flour your hands and work the mixture until it forms a soft, doughy ball. Wrap it in clingfilm and rest in the refrigerator for around 4 hours.

3. Preheat the oven to 200°C/fan 180°C/gas mark 6. With floured hands, roll walnut-sized pieces of the dough into smooth balls. Place the balls roughly 2.5cm (1in) apart on a baking sheet lined with nonstick baking paper. Using your thumb, press a hole into the centre of each cookie (but not right through). Gently smooth over any cracks that appear in the dough. Bake the cookies for 10 minutes.

4. Remove the cookies from the oven and spoon a little jam into each thumbprint. Return to the oven and bake for a further 4 minutes, or until the cookies are pale golden. Leave to cool on the baking sheet for a few minutes, then transfer the cookies to a wire rack. Dust with icing sugar and leave to cool completely. (Don't worry about the icing sugar obscuring the colour of the jam – it comes through again once the icing sugar has sunk in.)

44

STRAWBERRY & MANGO SHORTCAKE

This shortcake really must be made the day you want to eat it and is best served as fresh as possible. It rises a lot at first, but don't worry: it does sink down again.

Serves 8

335g (11¾oz) plain flour,
  plus extra for flouring
1 tbsp baking powder
¾ tsp salt
55g (2oz) caster sugar
115g (4oz) cold unsalted butter,
  cut into small pieces
250ml (9fl oz) double cream

For the topping:
300g (10½oz) strawberries
caster sugar, to taste
300ml (½ pint) double cream
3–4 tbsp Greek yogurt (optional)
1 mango, peeled, stoned
  and sliced
icing sugar, for dusting

1. Preheat the oven to 210°C/fan 190°C/gas mark 6½. Place the flour, baking powder, salt, caster sugar and butter into a mixing bowl. Rub the butter into the dry ingredients with your hands until the mixture forms pea-sized lumps. Make a well in the centre and pour in the cream. Stir to combine, then form the mixture into a ball using your hands.

2. Turn out the dough onto a lightly floured surface and roll into a 22–24cm (8½–9½in) round. Carefully transfer to a floured baking sheet and bake for 20–25 minutes. Remove from the oven and leave to cool on the baking sheet for 20 minutes until it can be handled (it is fragile at first and falls apart easily), then transfer to a wire rack to cool completely.

3. To make the topping, hull the strawberries and halve or quarter them, depending on their size. (I like to sprinkle the strawberries with caster sugar and leave them for 15 minutes to draw out their juice.) Whip the cream to soft peaks and add enough sugar to satisfy your sweet tooth. Stir the yogurt into the cream — I like the tartness that Greek yogurt brings. Taste again for sweetness.

4. Spoon the whipped cream onto the shortcake and arrange the mango slices and strawberries on top. Dust lightly with icing sugar immediately before serving.

COCONUT BISCUITS

Makes 12

For the shortbread:
300g (10½oz) plain flour, plus extra for flouring
125g (4½oz) caster sugar
125g (4½oz) semolina
250g (9oz) unsalted butter, softened, plus extra for greasing

For the topping:
55g (2oz) desiccated coconut
3 tbsp condensed milk
1 tsp ground cinnamon
6 glacé cherries, halved

1. Whizz the shortbread ingredients together in a food processor, or rub them together using your fingertips, until they resemble fine breadcrumbs. Turn out onto a floured work surface and use your hands to bring the mixture together into a firm dough. Wrap the dough in clingfilm and place it in the refrigerator for about 30 minutes.

2. Divide the dough into 12 pieces. Roll each piece into a ball, then flatten them out into 9–10cm (3½–4in) circles on greased baking sheets. Pinch the circles to make points around the edges and prick all over with a fork. Press down with your thumb and make a slight indentation in the centre of each biscuit. Leave to chill in the refrigerator for 20 minutes.

3. Preheat the oven to 160°C/fan 140°C/gas mark 3. To make the topping, mix together the coconut, condensed milk and cinnamon. Remove the biscuits from the refrigerator and drop large teaspoons of the topping mixture into the centre of each biscuit.

4. Bake the biscuits for around 30–40 minutes, or until the shortbread is pale golden. Leave to cool on the baking sheets for a few minutes before transferring onto wire racks.

5. Press half a glacé cherry onto the centre of each biscuit and leave to cool completely.

EASY TO MAKE AND DELICIOUS!

TEXAN DOLLIES

300g (10½oz) digestive biscuits
200g (7oz) unsalted butter
140g (5oz) walnuts, chopped
85g (3oz) milk or dark chocolate chips
85g (3oz) sultanas
200g (7oz) desiccated coconut
600ml (1 pint) condensed milk
icing sugar, for dusting

Rich and over-the-top, these are for the seriously sweet-toothed, like me!

1. Preheat the oven to 180°C/fan 160°C/ gas mark 4. Place the biscuits in a sealed plastic bag and bash them with a rolling pin. Transfer to a bowl. Melt the butter and mix with the crumbs. Press the buttered crumbs into the bottom of a 20cm (8in) square, 5cm (2in) deep baking tin. Sprinkle over the walnuts, chocolate chips, sultanas and coconut. Pour over the condensed milk, spreading it evenly using palette knife.

2. Bake for 30—35 minutes or until golden around the edges. Take care not to overcook and leave to cool in the tin overnight.

3. Cut into squares (you'll need to use a sharp knife for this) and ease them out of the tin. Dust with icing sugar, then serve.

LIME BARS

A soft, shortbready base topped with lime-flavoured curd makes these bars truly luscious. Limes vary greatly in how much juice they produce, which is why I have put the quantity of juice rather than the quantity of limes you need. Make sure you select good ones by giving them a squeeze and rejecting any that feel hard. These squares are also good with dessicated or sweetened shaved coconut sprinkled on top.

Makes 30

250g (9oz) unsalted butter, softened, plus extra for greasing

90g (3¼oz) granulated sugar

250g (9oz) plain flour, plus extra for flouring

pinch of salt

icing sugar, for dusting

For the filling:

6 extra-large free-range eggs, at room temperature

625g (1lb 6oz) granulated sugar

finely grated rind of 8 unwaxed limes, plus extra for decorating

150ml (¼ pint) lime juice

125g (4½oz) plain flour

1. Preheat the oven to 190°C/fan 170°C/gas mark 5. Beat the butter and sugar together, using an electric mixer or by hand, until pale but not too fluffy. With the mixer set on a very low speed, add the flour and salt and beat gently until just combined. Turn out the dough (it may not have come together into a ball yet — don't worry) onto a lightly floured work surface and knead into a ball. Using well-floured hands, press the dough into a greased 30 × 22cm (12 × 8½in) rectangular baking tin. Chill in the refrigerator for 30 minutes (or stick it in the freezer for about 10 minutes).

2. Bake for 15—20 minutes until pale golden, then remove from the oven but don't turn the oven off. Leave to cool in the tin.

3. To make the filling, whisk together the eggs, sugar, lime rind and juice. When combined, gradually mix in the flour, whisking continuously. Pour into the cooled tin, on top of the cooled shortbread base, and bake for 30 minutes or until the filling is set. Leave to cool in the tin.

4. Cut into 30 small bars, dust with icing sugar and decorate with lime rind.

COCONUT RICE BARS

I love rice bars to snack on and these ones have coconut and honey in them to dub them up and make them special in a Caribbean way.

Makes 16

397g can condensed milk
50g (1¾oz) unsalted butter,
   plus extra for greasing
50g (1¾oz) clear honey
100g (3½oz) puffed rice cereal
60g (2¼oz) desiccated coconut,
   plus extra for decorating

1. Heat the condensed milk, butter and honey in a small saucepan set over a medium heat until the butter has melted, stirring occasionally. Cook for a further 10 minutes until the mixture turns into a light caramel, stirring often.

2. Remove the caramel from the heat and add the puffed rice cereal and coconut. Stir to combine, then tip into a greased 20cm (8in) square baking tin that is at least 7cm (2¾in) deep. Leave to cool for 30 minutes, then cut into 16 small squares. Decorate the top of each with a little sprinkle of coconut.

GINGER THINS

These elegant biscuits look fabulocious and you can do your thing with the slivers of ginger to decorate the top. Kids may want to make faces!

Makes 12

2 free-range egg whites
100g (3½oz) caster sugar
50g (1¾oz) unsalted butter,
   melted
finely grated rind of 1
   unwaxed lime
50g (1¾oz) plain flour
1½ tsp ground ginger
1 piece of preserved stem ginger
   in syrup, cut into slivers

1. Preheat the oven to 190°C/fan 170°C/gas mark 5. Whisk the egg whites until soft peaks form, then add the sugar and whisk again briefly. Add half each of the butter, lime rind, flour and ground ginger, beating well after each addition, then repeat with the remaining butter, lime rind, flour and ground ginger.

2. Spoon tablespoons of the mixture onto two lined baking sheets, leaving a small gap between each one. Spread each spoonful into thin rounds measuring around 9cm (3½in) diameter and 3mm (⅛in) thick. Scatter over the stem ginger slivers.

3. Bake for 6–8 minutes, or until brown around the edges. Leave to cool on the baking sheet for a couple of minutes, then use a palette knife to transfer the biscuits to a wire rack and leave to cool completely. Serve on their own, with tea or coffee, or with ice cream for a special treat.

CHOCOLATE & GINGER TIFFIN

A superior chocolate biscuit cake. Ginger, nuts sultanas, chocolate – how can we go wrong?!

Serves 8

225g (8oz) ginger biscuits
150g (5½oz) unsalted butter
2 tbsp golden syrup
1½ tbsp cocoa powder
75g (3oz) almonds or hazelnuts, toasted and roughly chopped
50g (1¾oz) sultanas
150g (5½oz) dark chocolate

1. Pulse the biscuits in a food processor or, alternatively, place them in a sealed plastic bag and bash them with a rolling pin until they are a mixture of completely crushed biscuits and small chunks.

2. Line a 15cm (6in) square baking tin or plastic container with foil or nonstick baking paper, ensuring that the lining extends over the edges of the tin so, later, you can easily lift the tiffin out of the tin once it has set.

3. Melt the butter and the syrup together in a heavy-based saucepan set over a medium heat. Add the cocoa powder, nuts and sultanas and stir until everything comes together. Press the mixture into the tin so it is around 3cm (1¼in) thick once flattened out. Leave to cool, then refrigerate until set.

4. Melt the dark chocolate in a bowl set over a pan of simmering water, ensuring that the base of the bowl doesn't touch the water. Pour the chocolate over the tiffin and leave to set (put it in the refrigerator to speed it up if you like).

5. Once completely hard, lift the tiffin out of the tin, holding onto the foil or baking paper. To serve, cut the tiffin into small squares with a sharp knife.

LEVI'S FAVOURITE FRIDGE BAR

This bar is a wicked infusion of energy. Listed below is my personal choice of chocolate bars – I know you will have your own favourites. When making this, you will have to cut off the ends of some of the chocolate bars to make them fit and – whoops! – you will have to eat the trimmings.

Serves 10

200g (7oz) dark chocolate
50g (1¾oz) unsalted butter
150ml (¼ pint) milk
2 tbsp dark rum
My choice of chocolate bars:
    2 × 37g bags of Maltesers
    1⅕ × 40g bars of Crunchie
    1½ × 57g bars of Bounty
    1 × 34g bar of Flake
    3 × 22g bars of Milky Way
    1½ × 38g packets of Smarties

1. Melt the dark chocolate together with the butter, milk and rum in a bowl set over a saucepan of simmering water, ensuring that the base of the bowl doesn't touch the water. Stir to combine, then remove from the heat and leave to cool slightly.

2. Put the Maltesers in the bottom of a 600ml (1 pint) loaf tin to cover the base. Pour over enough of the melted dark chocolate mixture to cover the Maltesers. Tap the tin firmly on the work surface a couple of times to release any air bubbles and distribute the chocolate mixture evenly.

3. Lay the Crunchies, Bounties and Flake on top of the chocolate, fitting them in one layer. Cut the Milky Ways in half lengthways and lay them on top of the other bars. Pour over the remaining chocolate mixture and tap the tin firmly on the work surface. Cover the top of the tin with clingfilm and put this chocolate feast in the refrigerator to set for at least 2 hours.

4. Keep in the refrigerator until ready to eat. To serve, dip the tin briefly into very hot water for around 10 seconds. Slip a knife around the edges and turn out this mighty chocolate-bar refrigerator cake onto a serving plate. Put 10 rows of Smarties on top of the chocolate, which will be slightly melted. Serve in slices with a row of Smarties per person.

PIES & TARTS

MANGO TARTE TATIN

Tarte Tatin is such a delicious pud, with caramelized fruit on top of buttery pastry. The brown-sugaring of the fruit can seem tricky, but you soon get the hang of the technique.

Serves 8

3 ripe mangos

juice of 1 lime

125g (4½oz) unsalted butter, softened

125g (4½oz) caster sugar

200g (7oz) sheet ready-made all-butter puff pastry

plain flour, for flouring

crème fraîche, to serve

1. Preheat the oven to 220°C/fan 200°C/gas mark 7. Peel and stone the mangos and cut the flesh lengthways into thick slices, then dip the slices into the lime juice.

2. Spread the butter evenly over the base of a 23cm (9in) diameter heavy-based ovenproof frying pan. Sprinkle over the sugar and arrange the mango slices on top. Heat the pan over a medium-high heat for 10—15 minutes, or until the butter and sugar have caramelized, moving the pan around from time to time to get the contents browning evenly. When the sugar and butter mixture is as brown as you dare (and remember that the mixture will keep cooking after it is removed from the heat), take the pan off the heat.

3. Roll out the puff pastry sheet on a lightly floured surface to a 25cm (10in) round. Place this on top of the mango, tucking the edges down around it, remembering that the mixture and the pan will be hot. Bake for 15 minutes, or until the pastry is brown and well risen. Leave to cool for a couple of minutes.

4. Put a plate on top of the pastry and, in one swoop, turn it upside down. Everything should come away onto the plate in one go but, if not, ease it out with a knife. Serve in slices with dollops of crème fraîche.

63

SPICED PLUM TART

This is such an easy tart to make – you don't have to line a tin and if your pastry breaks, just patch it up. You can even change the type of nuts or use the same amount of breadcrumbs instead.

Serves 8

150g (5½oz) cold unsalted
   butter, cut into small pieces
250g (9oz) plain flour, plus
   extra for flouring
70g (2½oz) icing sugar
1 free-range egg yolk
1 tbsp cold water
450g (1lb) plums, halved
   and stoned
85g (3oz) ground hazelnuts
35g (1¼oz) light soft brown
   sugar
½ tsp ground cinnamon
½ tsp ground ginger
35g (1¼oz) demerara sugar,
   plus extra for sprinkling
whipped cream, to serve

1. Place the butter, flour and icing sugar in a food processor and, using the pastry blade, whizz until the mixture resembles fine breadcrumbs. Mix the egg yolk with the water and pour into the food processor. Whizz again – the mixture should come together into a ball, although you may need to add a little more cold water to help bring it together. (Alternatively, put the butter and flour in a large bowl and rub together with your fingertips until the mixture resembles breadcrumbs. Stir in the icing sugar, then add the egg yolk and water. Bring the dough together into a ball with your hands.)

2. Wrap the dough in clingfilm and place in the refrigerator to chill for 30 minutes. Meanwhile cut the plums into 5mm (¼in) slices.

3. Preheat the oven to 210°C/fan 190°C/gas mark 6½. Roll out the dough on a lightly floured surface in a 25cm (10in) round and place it on a baking sheet. Mix the hazelnuts, brown sugar and spices together and sprinkle over the pastry, leaving a rim of 4cm (1½in) around the edge. Place the fruit on top in a higgledy-piggledy way and scatter with demerara sugar.

4. Pull the rim of the dough up over the fruit around the edges and sprinkle with demerara sugar. Bake for 30 minutes or until the plums are tender and the pastry is golden. (If the pastry is getting too dark but the fruit isn't cooked, cover the tart with foil.) Leave to cool, then serve lukewarm with whipped cream.

APRICOT & HONEY SQUARES

These are topped with one of my favourite fruits – luscious apricots – and the honey brings out their flavour even more. Scatter the squares with toasted flaked almonds once you've glazed them, if you fancy.

Makes 16–20

100g (3½oz) cold unsalted
    butter, cut into small pieces
200g (7oz) plain flour
175g (6oz) caster sugar
pinch of salt
1 free-range egg yolk
1 tsp vanilla extract
650g (1lb 7oz) fresh apricots
2 tbsp granulated sugar
100g (3½oz) apricot jam
4 tbsp clear honey
1 tbsp water
25g (1oz) toasted flaked almonds
    (optional)

1. Whizz the butter and flour in a food processor until the mixture resembles fine breadcrumbs. Add the caster sugar and salt and briefly whizz again until just combined. Add the egg yolk and vanilla extract and whizz until the mixture comes together into a ball. (Alternatively, put the butter and flour in a large bowl and rub together with your fingertips until the mixture resembles breadcrumbs. Stir in the caster sugar and salt, then add the egg yolk and vanilla extract. Bring the dough together into a ball with your hands.) You shouldn't need any more liquid but you can add a drop of very cold water if the dough isn't coming together.

2. Wrap the dough in clingfilm and place in the refrigerator to chill for 30 minutes. Meanwhile, quarter and stone the apricots.

3. Preheat the oven to 200°C/fan 180°C/gas mark 6. Press the dough into a 20 × 30cm (8 × 12in) baking tin. Arrange the apricot quarters in rows on top of the dough, pressing them down lightly as you go. Sprinkle over the granulated sugar and bake for 45 minutes. Leave to cool in the tin.

4. Heat the jam, honey and water in a saucepan set over a medium heat, stirring, until you have a thick glaze. Spoon or brush the glaze over the apricots, then sprinkle with toasted almonds. Leave to set, then cut into squares.

Serves 8–10

For the pastry:

175g (6oz) cold unsalted butter,
  cut into small pieces

225g (8oz) plain flour, plus extra
  for flouring

100g (3½oz) ground almonds

85g (3oz) caster sugar

pinch of salt

1 free-range egg yolk

½ tbsp cold water

For the filling:

350g (12oz) mascarpone cheese

225g (8oz) fromage frais

finely grated rind and juice of 1
  unwaxed lemon

6 tbsp icing sugar (or to taste)

700g (1lb 9oz) fruit, such as: 1 small
  mango, 1 banana, 100g (3½oz) cape
  gooseberries, 8 plump strawberries,
  2 kiwi fruits and 200g (7oz) pineapple,
  cut into chunks (about half a small
  pineapple – you can buy it ready-
  prepared so there is no wastage)

1 tbsp lemon juice

To serve:

freshly grated nutmeg

icing sugar, for dusting

Exotic Fruit Tart

Make sure you are generous with the fruit in this dish – it should look abundant. It's best to get all the bits of the tart ready and assemble it just before serving, but it's very easy to put together at the last minute.

1. Whizz the butter, flour, ground almonds, sugar and salt in a food processor until the mixture resembles breadcrumbs. Add the egg yolk and water and whizz until the mixture comes together into a ball. (Alternatively, put the butter, flour and ground almonds in a large bowl and rub together with your fingertips until the mixture resembles breadcrumbs. Stir in the sugar and salt, then add the egg yolk and water. Bring the dough together into a ball with your hands.) Wrap the dough in clingfilm and chill in the refrigerator for 30 minutes.

2. Roll out the dough on a lightly floured surface and use it to line a 25cm (10in) diameter fluted loose-bottomed flan tin. (If the pastry falls apart, just press it into the tin.) Place the tin in the coldest part of the refrigerator for 45 minutes, or in the freezer for 15 minutes, to chill.

3. Preheat the oven to 220°C/fan 200°C/gas mark 7. Line the pastry case with nonstick baking paper, fill with baking beans and bake blind for 8 minutes. Remove the paper and beans and bake for a further 8–9 minutes. Leave the pastry case to cool in the tin, then carefully turn it out and transfer to a wire rack to cool completely.

4. Meanwhile, make the filling. Beat the mascarpone until smooth. Add the fromage frais, icing sugar, lemon rind and juice and stir to combine. Put this mixture into the refrigerator to firm up slightly, but don't let it get so cold that it sets.

5. Next, prepare the fruit. Peel and stone the mango. Cut the flesh into slices or chunks. (Use the flesh left on the stone for a smoothie or something else — you need really neat pieces for this tart.) Slice the banana and immediately cover it with the lemon juice to stop it going brown. Remove some of the smaller leaves from the cape gooseberries, but leave the larger ones (they just look pretty). Hull and halve or quarter the strawberries (depending on their size) and peel and slice the kiwi fruit.

6. Fill the cooled pastry case with the mascarpone mixture and arrange the fruit in a higgledly-piggledy fashion on top. Be really generous — this tart should look sumptuous and plentiful. To serve, sprinkle over a little nutmeg (it's very Carribean to add this flavour to fruit) and dust with icing sugar.

BOOZY PRUNE & ALMOND TART

Here's a very simple tart with a fantastic boozy kick. For a rum-soaked apricot and almond tart, just replace the prunes with fresh apricots.

Serves 6–8

For the pastry:
125g (4½oz) cold unsalted
    butter, cut into small pieces
250g (9oz) plain flour, plus
    extra for flouring
1½ tbsp caster sugar
1 tsp vanilla extract
1 free-range egg yolk

For the filling:
275g (9¾oz) stoned prunes
150ml (¼ pint) white or dark rum
2 free-range eggs
100g (3½oz) ground almonds
25g (1oz) unsalted butter, melted
125g (4½oz) golden caster sugar
150ml (¼ pint) double cream
icing sugar, or 3 tbsp apricot jam
    and 1 tbsp water, to finish
whipped cream, to serve

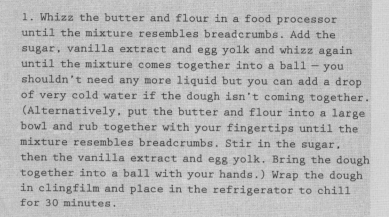

1. Whizz the butter and flour in a food processor until the mixture resembles breadcrumbs. Add the sugar, vanilla extract and egg yolk and whizz again until the mixture comes together into a ball — you shouldn't need any more liquid but you can add a drop of very cold water if the dough isn't coming together. (Alternatively, put the butter and flour into a large bowl and rub together with your fingertips until the mixture resembles breadcrumbs. Stir in the sugar, then the vanilla extract and egg yolk. Bring the dough together into a ball with your hands.) Wrap the dough in clingfilm and place in the refrigerator to chill for 30 minutes.

2. Roll out the dough on a lightly floured surface and use it to line a 24cm (9½in) diameter fluted loose-bottomed flan tin. Place the tin in the coldest part of the refrigerator for 45 minutes or in the freezer for 15 minutes to chill the pastry. Meanwhile, prepare the filling. Heat the prunes and rum in a saucepan set over a low heat until warm, without bringing the liquid to the boil. Remove from the heat and leave the prunes to soak in the warm alcohol for about 45 minutes.

3. Preheat the oven to 200°C/fan 180°C/gas mark 6. Beat the eggs in a bowl and whisk in the almonds, butter, sugar and cream. Add 3 tablespoons of the rum from the saucepan. Remove the prunes from the saucepan, shaking off any excess liquid, and place in the chilled pastry case in 2 concentric circles. Pour over the egg mixture and bake for 30 minutes or until the top is puffed up and golden. Leave to cool a little in the tin.

4. To finish, dust a little icing sugar over the top of the tart or glaze it with apricot jam. (To make a glaze, heat jam in a saucepan with a little water until it resembles a thick syrup. Brush over the tart, avoiding any lumps.) Serve with whipped cream.

GINGER & LIME TREACLE TART

You must try this dubbed-up classic. It's gorgeous to look at, lovely to eat, and just as good with a cup of tea as it is after an indulgent family meal.

Serves 6

For the pastry:

60g (2¼oz) cold unsalted butter, cut into small pieces

125g (4½oz) plain flour, plus extra for flouring

50g (1¾oz) icing sugar

1 free-range egg yolk

For the filling:

454g can golden syrup

finely grated rind of 2 unwaxed limes

2 pieces of preserved stem ginger in syrup, finely chopped

100g (3½oz) white breadcrumbs

whipped cream, to serve

1. To make the pastry, put the butter, flour and icing sugar into a food processor. Pulse briefly to combine. Add the egg yolk and pulse again until the mixture starts to come together. Tip the mixture into a bowl. (Alternatively, put the butter and flour into a large bowl and rub together with your fingertips until the mixture resembles breadcrumbs. Mix in the icing sugar, then the egg.) Bring the dough together in a ball with your hands. Wrap in clingfilm and chill in the refrigerator for 30 minutes.

2. Roll out the dough on a lightly floured surface and use it to line a 25cm (10in) diameter fluted loose-bottomed flan tin. Put the tin into the refrigerator for 20 minutes to chill. Meanwhile, preheat the oven to 200°C/fan 180°C/gas mark 6.

3. Line the pastry case with nonstick baking paper, fill with baking beans and bake blind for 15 minutes. Remove the paper and beans and bake for a further 5 minutes or until golden.

4. Meanwhile, make the filling. Heat the syrup in a small saucepan set over a low heat until loosened. Add the lime rind, ginger and breadcrumbs and stir to combine. Pour the mixture into the tart case and return to the oven for 15—20 minutes until lightly browned. Serve with a dollop of whipped cream.

Caribbean Bakewell Tart

Serves 8

For the pastry:

85g (3oz) cold unsalted butter,
    cut into small pieces

125g (4½oz) plain flour, plus
    extra for flouring

25g (1oz) caster sugar

1 free-range egg, separated

½ tbsp cold water

For the filling:

150g (5½oz) unsalted butter,
    softened

150g (5½oz) caster sugar

3 free-range eggs, beaten,
    plus 1 yolk

100g (3½oz) ground almonds

finely grated rind of 2
    unwaxed limes

1 tbsp white rum

3 tbsp lime marmalade

pouring cream, to serve

To finish:

handful of toasted flaked
    almonds or sweetened
    coconut shavings

icing sugar, for dusting

pouring cream, to serve

*Make this with mango jam instead
to give it a real Caribbean Kick!*

1. To make the pastry, put the butter, flour and sugar into a food processor and whizz until the mixture resembles breadcrumbs. Mix the egg yolk with the water and pour into the food processor. Whizz again until the pastry comes together into a ball. (Alternatively, put the butter and flour in a large bowl and rub together with your fingertips until the mixture resembles breadcrumbs. Stir in the sugar, then add the egg yolk and water. Bring the dough together into a ball with your hands.) Wrap it in clingfilm and chill in the refrigerator for 30 minutes.

2. Roll out the dough on a lightly floured surface and use it to line a 20cm (8in) diameter, 3.5cm (1½in) deep, fluted loose-bottomed flan tin. Put the tin into the freezer for 20 minutes to chill the pastry.

3. Meanwhile preheat the oven to 220°C/fan 200°C/gas mark 7. Line the pastry case with nonstick baking paper, fill with baking beans and bake blind for 15 minutes. Remove the paper and beans. Lightly whisk the egg white and paint the dough with it. Return the pastry case to the oven for 5 minutes, then remove. Reduce the heat to 200°C/fan 180°C/gas mark 6.

4. Now make the filling. Beat the butter and sugar together until pale and fluffy. Gradually add the beaten eggs plus the extra yolk, beating after each addition. Fold in the almonds, lime rind and rum.

5. Spread the base of the tart case with the marmalade, then spoon in the almond mixture and spread it out using the back of a spoon. (It will look like you don't have enough filling, but don't worry.) Bake for 35—40 minutes or until the filling is set and golden on top. Leave to cool, then scatter over the flaked almonds or coconut shavings and dust lightly with icing sugar. Serve with pouring cream.

Serves 8

For the pastry:

100g (3½oz) cold unsalted butter,
    cut into small pieces

200g (7oz) plain flour, plus extra
    for flouring

85g (3oz) icing sugar

1 free-range egg

For the filling:

5 free-range eggs

250g (9oz) light muscovado sugar

200g (7oz) golden syrup

pinch of salt

70g (2½oz) unsalted butter, melted

6 cloves, crushed

½ tsp grated nutmeg

1 tsp vanilla extract

3 tbsp plain flour

200g (7oz) pecans, half roughly chopped,
    half left whole

crème fraîche sprinkled with grated
    nutmeg, to serve

LEVI'S PECAN PIE

1. To make the pastry, rub the butter and flour together in a large bowl with your fingertips until the mixture resembles breadcrumbs. Mix in the icing sugar, then add the egg and mix to combine. Bring the dough together into a ball with your hands. Wrap in clingfilm and chill in the refrigerator for 30 minutes.

2. Roll out the dough on a lightly floured surface and use it to line a 30cm (12in) diameter fluted loose-bottomed flan tin. Patch up any tears in the dough with the trimmings, pressing these into the case firmly to prevent any of the filling leaking out later. Refrigerate for 20 minutes. Meanwhile, preheat the oven to 200°C/fan 180°C/gas mark 6.

3. Line the pastry case with nonstick baking paper, fill with baking beans and bake blind for 15 minutes. Remove the paper and beans and bake for 5 minutes more. Remove from the oven and reduce the heat to 190°C/fan 170°C/gas mark 5.

4. Meanwhile, make the filling. Beat the eggs in a bowl, then whisk in the sugar, golden syrup, salt, melted butter, cloves, nutmeg, vanilla extract and flour. Stir in the chopped pecans. Pour into the pastry case and arrange the whole pecans on top. Bake for 30 minutes or until just set. Serve with crème fraîche sprinkled with a little grated nutmeg.

PINEAPPLE & RUM FRANGIPANE TART

Frangipane is an almond paste that goes really well with pineapple. It takes a bit of time to peel a pineapple, not least because you have to take out the 'eyes', so for this tasty tart, using the canned variety is fine.

Serves 6

For the pastry:

60g (2¼oz) cold unsalted butter, cut into small pieces

125g (4½oz) plain flour, plus extra for flouring

50g (1¾oz) icing sugar

1 free-range egg yolk, beaten

For the frangipane:

85g (3oz) unsalted butter, softened

85g (3oz) light muscovado sugar

2 free-range eggs

2 tbsp dark rum

85g (3oz) ground almonds

1 tbsp plain flour

260g (9½oz) fresh or canned pineapple, sliced

4 tbsp apricot jam, to glaze

1 tbsp water

pouring cream, to serve

1. To make the pastry, put the butter, flour and icing sugar into a mixing bowl. Lightly rub the butter into the dry ingredients until the mixture resembles breadcrumbs. Add the egg yolk and mix until the dough comes together into a ball. Wrap the dough in clingfilm and chill in the refrigerator 30 minutes.

2. Roll out the pastry out on a lightly floured surface and use it to line a 25cm (10in) diameter fluted loose-bottomed flan tin. Refrigerate for 20 minutes to chill the dough.

3. Preheat the oven to 180°C/fan 160°C/gas mark 4. To make the frangipane, beat the butter and sugar together, using an electric mixer or by hand, until pale and fluffy. Add the eggs and rum and beat to combine. Fold in the ground almonds and flour. Spoon into the pastry case and spread out evenly. Arrange the pineapple slices on top in concentric circles. Bake for 25 minutes. Leave to cool for 10 minutes, then turn the tart out onto a serving plate.

4. Heat the apricot jam in a saucepan with the water until it resembles a thick syrup. Either push this through a sieve then spoon it over the tart, or brush it on carefully, avoiding any lumps of apricot. Serve the tart warm or cold with cream.

LIME & GINGER PIE

This American-inspired tart is great for celebrating Independence Day. Use good juicy limes – give them a squeeze when you're buying them and reject any that feel hard, as they won't be juicy.

1. Preheat the oven to 200°C/fan 180°C/gas mark 6. Whizz the biscuits into crumbs in a food processor, or put them in a plastic bag and bash them with a rolling pin. Transfer to a bowl. Melt the butter gently in a pan set over a low heat, then mix it into the biscuit crumbs. Press the buttered crumbs into a 23cm (9in) pie dish to cover the base and sides. Bake for 10 minutes or until firm. Leave to cool completely, but don't turn off the oven.

2. Meanwhile, make the filling. Beat the egg yolks until they are creamy and golden. Stir in the condensed milk, lime juice and rind and mix well until smooth. Pour into the cooled pie base and bake for 15–20 minutes or until the filling is just set. You can decorate the pie with swirls of whipped cream, but I prefer it left plain and simple. Offer some whipped cream on the side, though, and serve with berries — a mixture of blueberries and raspberries is perfect.

Serves 10

280g (10oz) ginger biscuits
125g (4½oz) unsalted butter

For the filling:
4 free-range egg yolks
2 × 397g cans condensed milk
150ml (¼ pint) lime juice
rind of 5 unwaxed limes

To serve:
whipped cream
mixed berries

SALTED CARAMEL CHEESECAKE

1. To make the ginger base, whizz the biscuits into crumbs in a food processor, or put them in a sealed plastic bag and bash them with a rolling pin. Transfer to a bowl. Melt the butter in a pan set over a low heat, then mix it into the crumbs. Press the buttered crumbs into a 22cm (8½in) diameter round loose-bottomed cake tin, pushing the mixture up the sides by a couple of centimetres (about an inch) to make a slight rim. Chill the base in the refrigerator until firm.

2. To make the salted caramel, heat the condensed milk, butter and sugar in a small saucepan set over a medium heat, stirring continuously until the butter melts. Simmer for 5 minutes over a low heat, stirring continuously, until thick and of a light caramel colour. Stir in the salt but don't taste it until it's cool! Spread the cooled caramel over the ginger base in an even layer. Refrigerate until cool.

3. To make the filling, whip the cream until it is firm but not too stiff. Mash the cream cheese with a fork, then add it to the cream and whisk to combine. Spread evenly over the caramel layer and chill in the refrigerator.

4. To make the lime jelly topping, soak the gelatine leaves in water for 5 minutes. Meanwhile, mix the lime juice and sugar together in a small saucepan and gently heat until the sugar has dissolved. Remove from the heat. Squeeze the gelatine to remove any excess water and add it to the saucepan. Stir until it has dissolved, then add the lime rind. Leave to cool and then refrigerate for 15–20 minutes or until it begins to turn to jelly.

5. Spoon the lime jelly over the cheesecake and refrigerate until ready to serve.

Serves 8–12

For the ginger base:
300g (10½oz) ginger biscuits
125g (4½oz) unsalted butter

For the salted caramel:
½ × 397g can condensed milk
70g (2½oz) unsalted butter
30g (1⅛oz) light muscovado sugar
¼ tsp sea salt

For the filling:
300ml (½ pint) whipping cream
300g (10½oz) cream cheese

For the lime jelly topping:
2 small leaves of gelatine (weighing 3.3g in total)
125ml (4fl oz) lime juice
2 tbsp caster sugar
finely grated rind of 1 unwaxed lime

I buy a lot of cheesecake when I'm out and about. This one is really good to make at home and it's fine to make it the day before you want to serve it.

CREAMY
Puds

FRUITS AND NUTS

PLATE XIII.

1. ½ Nat. Size. 2. ½ Nat. Size. 3. ½ Nat. Size. 4. ½ Nat. Size. 7. ½ Nat. Size. 5. ½ Nat. Size. 6. ½ Nat. Size. 8. ½ Nat. Size. 9. ½ Nat. Size. 10. ½ Nat. Size.

1. GUAVA. 2. JUJUBE. 3. MANGOSTEEN. 4. LITCHI. 5. PISTACIA. 6. AVOCADO PEAR.
7. DURIO. 8. MALAY APPLE. 9. AKEE FRUITS AND NUTS. 10. MANGO.

BLACKIE & SON, GLASGOW, EDINBURGH & LONDON.

This is traditional English Eton Mess given a good dubbing up! The meringues go soft if they sit around, so serve it straight away. I visited the famous school, Eton College, once for one of the maddest talks I've ever done. The room was packed to the rafters and those boys had my Reggae Reggae Sauce all over them by the end. This recipe is dedicated to them.

Serves 8

2 small ripe bananas

juice of ½ lime

275ml (9½fl oz) double cream

2 pieces of preserved stem ginger in syrup, finely chopped, plus 1 tbsp syrup

6 tbsp Greek yogurt

5 tbsp icing sugar

400g (14oz) strawberries, hulled and quartered

200g (7oz) meringue shells, crushed

1. Peel and slice the bananas, put them in a bowl and cover them with the lime juice to stop them from discolouring. Whip the cream until stiff and stir in the ginger (reserving a little for decoration), ginger syrup, yogurt and icing sugar.

2. Add the banana and lime juice to the cream, along with the strawberries and crushed meringue, reserving a little to decorate. Carefully mix to combine.

3. Spoon the pudding into dessert glasses and decorate with the reserved ginger and meringue. Serve immediately.

85

JAMAICAN TIRAMISU

The Italian classic can hardly be bettered – except by the addition of rum. Tiramisu is translated as 'pick me up', but this is more of a 'lay-me-down-and-let-me-go-to-sleep' kind of pudding!

1. Whisk the cream, mascarpone and sugar together until well combined. Gradually add the rum and the Tia Maria, whisking after each addition.

2. Pour the coffee into a shallow dish and dip in the sponge fingers, one at a time, until they are damp but not soggy or falling apart. Lay half of the sponge fingers in the base of a serving dish, then spread half of the cream mixture on top. Sprinkle over the chocolate.

3. Lay over the remaining sponge fingers and cream mixture. Cover with clingfilm and refrigerate until ready to serve (it will keep at this stage for up to 2 days).

4. To decorate, cut two strips of nonstick baking paper about 2.5cm (1in) wide and lay them at angles over the top of the tiramisu. Dust with cocoa powder, then carefully remove the paper and serve.

Serves 8

- 400ml (14fl oz) double cream
- 500g (1lb 2oz) mascarpone cheese
- 8 tbsp soft light brown sugar
- 50ml (2fl oz) white or dark rum
- 30ml (1fl oz) Tia Maria
- 350ml (12fl oz) very strong coffee
- 175g (6oz) sponge fingers
- 100g (3½oz) dark chocolate, coarsely grated
- cocoa powder, to decorate

GINGER & PEAR TRIFLE

When you make a trifle you do your own thing – it should be about you. Add whatever ingredients you fancy and serve the pud how you like. You can make one big trifle in a bowl or use small glasses or bowls. Either way, it's going to taste wonderful! If you don't have time to make the custard, use 600ml (1 pint) ready-made custard mixed with 4 tbsp ginger syrup instead.

Serves 10

265g ready-made ginger cake, such as Levi Roots Jamaican Ginger Cake

85g (3oz) rhubarb and ginger jam

2 tbsp ginger wine

2 × 410g cans pears, drained and juice reserved

good grating of nutmeg

250ml (9fl oz) whipping cream

1½ pieces of preserved stem ginger in syrup, sliced, to decorate

For the ginger and muscovado custard:

300ml (½ pint) milk

300ml (½ pint) double cream

6 free-range egg yolks

3 tbsp light muscovado sugar

4 tbsp ginger syrup (from the jar of preserved stem ginger)

1 tsp vanilla extract

2 tbsp cornflour

1. To make the ginger and muscovado custard, heat the milk and cream in a saucepan set over a medium heat until almost boiling, then remove from the heat. Meanwhile whisk the egg yolks with the sugar, ginger syrup and vanilla extract.

2. Mix 4 tbsp of the milk and cream mixture with the cornflour to form a paste, then add this to the egg yolk mixture. Add the remaining milk and cream mixture, whisking to combine. Return the pan to a medium-low heat and cook, stirring continuously, for 6 minutes or until the mixture thickens. If the mixture starts to curdle, whisk briskly to bring the mixture together (you can sieve out any lumps). Leave the custard to cool. (Alternatively omit steps 1 and 2 and, instead, stir 4 tablespoons of ginger syrup into ready-made custard.)

3. Cut the ginger cake into 10 slices and spread each slice with rhubarb and ginger jam. Prick the slices all over with a fork and cut each into quarters, then place the cake in a serving bowl.

4. Mix the ginger wine with 100ml (3½fl oz) of the reserved pear juice, drinking the remainder, and pour this over the cake. Slice the pears and layer them over the cake, then pour over the custard. Grate over nutmeg, to taste, to give the dish that extra magic. Chill the trifle in the refrigerator. (You can make it the day before serving, but don't add the whipped cream until just before eating.)

5. To serve, whisk the cream into soft peaks and spoon around the edges of the trifle. Decorate with the stem ginger slices.

VANILLA RICE PUDDING WITH CHERRY & RUM SYRUP

Rice pudding is one of those real comfort foods. The amount of rice in this recipe looks tiny, but as it bakes in the oven it swells to fill the dish. Instead of serving this variation with a dollop of jam, I've created a beautiful cherry and rum syrup to swirl over the top.

Serves 6

100g (3½oz) pudding rice

150ml (¼ pint) double cream

500ml (18fl oz) milk

25g (1oz) caster sugar

pinch of salt

1 vanilla pod

For the cherry and rum syrup:

2 tbsp dark rum

100ml (3½fl oz) water

2 tbsp dark or light muscovado sugar

100g (3½oz) dried cherries

1. Preheat the oven to 160°C/fan 140°C/gas mark 3. Mix together the rice, cream, milk, sugar and salt. Cut the vanilla pod in half and use a knife to scrape out the seeds, then add these to the rice mixture. (If you like, put the vanilla pod in as well to add a little more flavour.) Pour the mixture into a 25—30cm (10—12in) diameter ovenproof dish and bake for 2 hours.

2. Meanwhile, make the syrup. Heat all of the ingredients in a small saucepan set over a medium heat. Bring to the boil, then reduce the heat and cook until the cherries have absorbed all of the liquid, stirring occasionally.

3. Leave the rice pudding to cool a little, then serve warm or cold with the cherry and rum syrup.

MANGO & PASSION FRUIT JELLIES

Kids love these jellies and you can get them involved in making them.

Serves 8

8 passion fruit

juice of 2 limes

750ml–1 litre (1⅓–1¾ pints)
    mango and apple juice

12 small leaves of gelatine
    (weighing 20g in total)

4 tbsp caster sugar

To serve:
250ml (9fl oz) whipping cream

icing sugar, to taste

1. Halve the passion fruit and scoop the pulp and juice into a sieve sat over a measuring jug. Push the juice through with the back of a spoon, reserving the pulp and seeds. Add the lime juice and enough mango and apple juice to make the quantity up to 1.2 litres (2 pints).

2. Put the gelatine in a shallow bowl, cover with water and set aside. Transfer the juice mixture to a small saucepan, stir in the sugar and heat until just below boiling point. Remove from the heat. Squeeze the excess water out of the gelatine sheets. Add them to the saucepan. Stir to melt the gelatine and set aside to cool.

3. Pour the jelly into 8 pretty glasses or metal jelly moulds and refrigerate until set. Whip the cream to soft peaks, adding icing sugar to taste. To serve, spoon a swirl of cream on top of each jelly and then top with the reserved passion-fruit pulp and seeds.

Serve with cream

BANANA & CHOCOLATE RUM SUNDAE

Banana splits are all very well, but I like fruit layered up with my chocolate sauce. And what a great sauce this is! Use it for drizzling over ice creams, warm crêpes and chocolate cake.

Serves 8

3 large or 4 small ripe bananas
juice of 1 lemon
175ml (6fl oz) whipping cream
icing sugar, to taste
2 tbsp dark rum
500ml (18fl oz) tub vanilla
     or almond ice cream

For the chocolate sauce:
200g (7oz) dark chocolate
100ml (3½fl oz) milk
50ml (2fl oz) double cream
40g (1½oz) caster sugar
25g (1oz) unsalted butter
dark rum, to taste

To serve:
handful of chopped pecans
8 wafer biscuits

1. Peel and thickly slice the bananas, place them in a bowl and immediately pour over the lemon juice to prevent them discolouring.

2. To make the chocolate sauce, melt the chocolate in a bowl set over a saucepan of simmering water, ensuring that the base of the bowl doesn't touch the water. Meanwhile, heat the milk, cream and sugar in a saucepan set over a medium heat, stirring frequently, until the sugar has dissolved.

3. Add the milk mixture to the warm chocolate, a little at a time, whisking between each addition (at first it will look as if the chocolate and milk mixture won't combine, but keep beating and it will all come together). Add the butter and allow it to melt into the sauce. Leave the sauce to cool to lukewarm, then stir in some rum to taste.

4. Whip the cream to soft peaks and add icing sugar to taste. Stir in the rum.

5. To assemble the sundaes, layer scoops of ice cream with the bananas and chocolate sauce in tall glasses and add a dollop of cream to each. Serve immediately, sprinkled with the chopped pecans and accompanied by wafer biscuits.

Ginger Toffee-apple Sundae

Mmmm – another lip-smacking sundae! Serve this one around an autumn bonfire to make your Guy Fawkes celebrations go with a bang!

Serves 6

4 tart eating apples
  (such as Granny Smiths)

35g (1¼oz) unsalted butter

1 tbsp caster sugar

500g (1lb 2oz) vanilla or ginger
  ice cream

50g (1¾oz) hazelnuts, chopped
  and toasted

For the toffee sauce:

150g (5½oz) soft light brown
  sugar

100g (3½oz) unsalted butter

1 tbsp golden syrup

1 piece of preserved stem ginger
  in syrup, plus 4 tbsp syrup

75ml (2½fl oz) ginger wine

1. To make the toffee sauce, heat the sugar, butter and golden syrup in a heavy-based saucepan over a low heat, stirring occasionally until the sugar has dissolved. Meanwhile, finely chop the stem ginger.

2. Increase the heat and add the stem ginger, ginger syrup and ginger wine. Whisk to combine. Bring to the boil and allow to simmer for a couple of minutes before removing from the heat. Set aside. (The sauce should be warm when served so you can make it ahead of time and gently heat it just before assembling the sundaes.)

3. Peel, halve and core the apples and cut them into slices. Melt the butter in a large frying pan set over a medium heat and add the apple slices. Sauté the apples on both sides until they are just tender but still retain their shape. Add the sugar and toss it with the apples until slightly caramelized and dark gold.

4. Quickly layer the ice cream in sundae glasses with the apples, hazelnuts (reserving some nuts to decorate) and toffee sauce. Sprinkle over the reserved hazelnuts and serve immediately.

Coconut Cloud

I wanted to make a coconut mousse in a coconut shell – it ended up looking like a big cloud in the sky, hence the name! If you add plenty of chilli, then you've got a Coconut Storm Cloud. Either way, it's certainly a moreish mousse. You can buy either pieces of fresh coconut or a whole one and prepare it yourself – that way you'll have the shell to serve the mousse in.

Serves 6

125g (4½oz) fresh coconut pieces, plus extra to decorate, or 1 whole coconut

½ tsp freshly grated nutmeg, or to taste

¼ tsp chilli powder, or to taste (optional)

250ml (9fl oz) whipping cream

150g (5½oz) ready-made custard

2 tbsp icing sugar, or to taste

1. If using a whole coconut, first drain the juice. Use a small sharp knife to discover which of the three holes on the top of the coconut is the real one (it was a game to have to guess this when I was a boy). Push down into the hole with the tip of the knife, then pour the juice into a glass to drink; in Jamaica this drink is called 'heart juice', because it's so good for you.

2. Now break the coconut in half by banging it down on a hard surface, such as a patio. You want to hit it on the 'equator', or widest part. Carefully prise the flesh out of the shell using the knife, then clean the shell ready for serving.

3. Finely grate the coconut flesh and mix with the nutmeg, and the chilli, if using. Whip the cream into soft peaks and mix it with the custard, then add the icing sugar and fold in the spicy coconut. Add more nutmeg, chilli and icing sugar to taste, if you like.

4. Dollop the 'cloud' into the coconut shell, if using, or into a bowl, then decorate with coconut shavings before serving.

MOCHA POTS

Coffee is good, and chocolate is even better, so what could be nicer than to put them together! These superlicious pots are even easier to make than chocolate mousse. Make sure you use good-quality dark chocolate, with a minimum of 70 percent cocoa solids, for the tastiest result.

Serves 6

4 tbsp soft light brown sugar
2 tbsp cornflour
4 tsp good quality ground coffee
250ml (9fl oz) milk
250ml (9fl oz) double cream
200g (7oz) dark chocolate,
    broken into pieces
25g (1oz) unsalted butter
1 tsp vanilla extract
coffee beans, to decorate

To serve:
250ml (9fl oz) whipping cream
2 tbsp icing sugar, or to taste

1. Place the sugar, cornflour and coffee into a saucepan. Gradually add the milk and cream, whisking after each addition to prevent lumps from forming. Place the saucepan over a medium heat and bring to the boil, stirring the mixture continuously, until the mixture thickens, then remove from the heat.

2. Add the chocolate to the saucepan along with the butter and vanilla extract. Whisk the mixture until the chocolate has melted and the mixture is completely smooth. Divide the mixture between 6 ramekin dishes or small coffee cups, cover with clingfilm and refrigerate for 2 hours, or until the mousse is firm.

3. Decorate the mocha pots with coffee beans. Carefully whisk the cream and icing sugar to soft peaks and serve this in a jug alongside the pots so people can help themselves.

MANGO & MASCARPONE FOOL

Dried mango is a great snack and makes a quick and easy fool when combined with double cream and rich mascarpone. If you like, you can decorate this with fresh mango, too.

Serves 8

150g (5½oz) dried mango

400ml (14fl oz) mango and
    passion-fruit juice

4 tbsp soft light brown sugar

2 tbsp lime juice

300ml (½ pint) double cream

250g (9oz) mascarpone cheese

1 fresh mango, to serve
    (optional)

1. Place the dried mango in a bowl, pour over the mango and passion-fruit juice and leave to soak for 30 minutes.

2. Transfer the dried mango and juice to a liquidizer, add the sugar and lime juice and whizz to a purée.

3. Whisk the cream to soft peaks, then fold in the mascarpone, then the mango purée. Spoon the fool into a serving dish and refrigerate until ready to serve.

4. To serve, peel and stone the mango, if using, and slice the flesh lengthways. Decorate the mousse with the mango slices.

ROAST APPLE, RUM & MAPLE FOOL

Wow, this is GOOD! To save time, you can just chop the apple flesh and cook it in a pan on the hob, but roasting gives it a special toffee flavour.

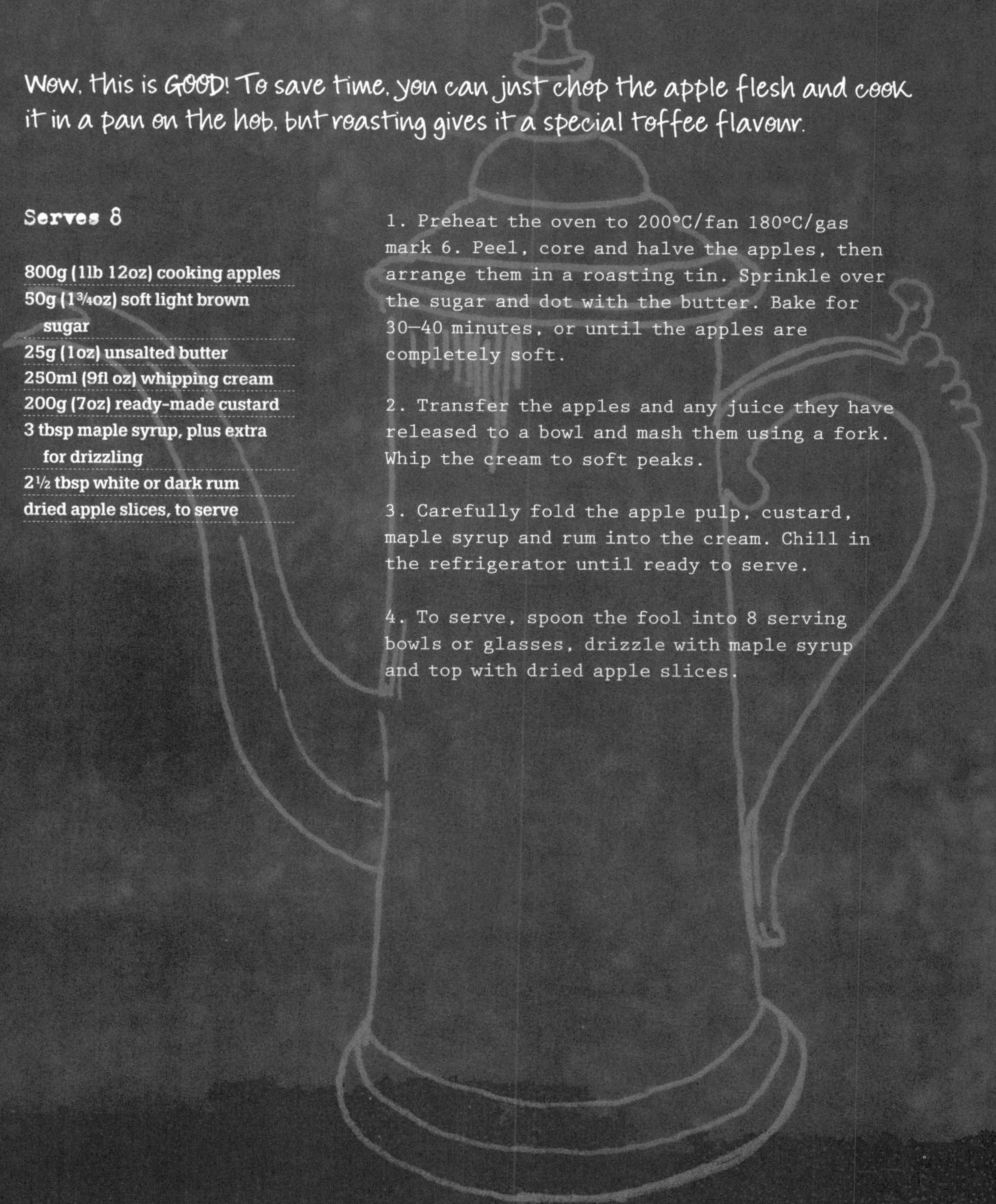

Serves 8

800g (1lb 12oz) cooking apples

50g (1¾oz) soft light brown sugar

25g (1oz) unsalted butter

250ml (9fl oz) whipping cream

200g (7oz) ready-made custard

3 tbsp maple syrup, plus extra for drizzling

2½ tbsp white or dark rum

dried apple slices, to serve

1. Preheat the oven to 200°C/fan 180°C/gas mark 6. Peel, core and halve the apples, then arrange them in a roasting tin. Sprinkle over the sugar and dot with the butter. Bake for 30—40 minutes, or until the apples are completely soft.

2. Transfer the apples and any juice they have released to a bowl and mash them using a fork. Whip the cream to soft peaks.

3. Carefully fold the apple pulp, custard, maple syrup and rum into the cream. Chill in the refrigerator until ready to serve.

4. To serve, spoon the fool into 8 serving bowls or glasses, drizzle with maple syrup and top with dried apple slices.

CARIBBEAN CRANACHAN

My real surname is Graham, a legacy of the Scottish slave masters in Jamaica who passed their name to their offspring. Cranachan is a classic Scots pudding, but this version, like me, is a mixture of Scottish and Caribbean, as it uses rum instead of whisky.

Serves 8

25g (1oz) porridge oats
1 small ripe banana
300ml (½ pint) double cream
3 tbsp white rum
6 tbsp clear honey,
     plus extra for drizzling
200g (7oz) raspberries

1. Toast the oats in a dry frying pan, taking care not to burn them. Transfer to a plate and set aside to cool. Meanwhile, peel and slice the banana.

2. Whip the cream to soft peaks, then fold in the rum, honey, oats, raspberries and banana, reserving a few of the raspberries and toasted oats for decoration.

3. Spoon the cranachan into 8 dessert glasses. Decorate with the reserved raspberries and oats and drizzle over a little honey.

BAKED & STEAMED

Puds

UITHEEMSE FRUITSOORTEN
4. DE ANANAS - DE KAKI
LIEBIG PRODUKTEN = besparing
Nadruk verboden   Verklaring op keerzijde

UITHEEMSE FRUITSOORTEN
4. DE ANANAS - DE KAKI
LIEBIG PRODUKTEN = besparing
Nadruk verboden   Verklaring op keerzijde

3♥

In 1892 Captain John Kidwell, an
English horticulturalist, was the first
to can pineapple.

♥3

PLAYER'S CIGARETTES.

PINE-APPLES.

This recipe looks a bit 1970s retro with the brown sugar and pineapple on top, but the taste sure doesn't date – it's still delicious! I like to put chilli in the middle of each pineapple ring, instead of the traditional retro glacé cherry.

Serves 8

175g (6oz) unsalted butter, softened
175g (6oz) caster sugar
175g (6oz) self-raising flour
1½ tsp baking powder
50g (1¾oz) ground almonds
4 free-range eggs
2 tsp vanilla extract
4 tbsp juice from pineapple can, if needed
pouring cream or ice cream, to serve

For the topping:
85g (3oz) unsalted butter, softened, plus extra for greasing
85g (3oz) soft light brown sugar
432g can pineapple rings in juice
1 red chilli, sliced widthways

1. Preheat the oven to 180°C/fan 160°C/ gas mark 4. To make the topping, beat the butter and sugar together, using an electric mixer or by hand, until pale and fluffy, and use the mixture to cover the base of a 25cm (10in) diameter round loose-bottomed cake tin. Grease the sides of the tin and arrange the pineapple rings on top of the butter and sugar mixture. Place a slice of chilli into the centre of each pineapple ring.

2. To make the cake, beat the butter and sugar together, using an electric mixer or by hand, until pale and fluffy. In a separate bowl, mix together the flour, baking powder and ground almonds.

3. Add the eggs to the butter and sugar mixture one at a time, alternating with spoonfuls of the dry ingredients, and beat with the mixer set on a low speed, or stir gently by hand, after each addition. Once combined, stir in the vanilla extract and add the pineapple juice, if necessary, to achieve a dropping consistency.

4. Spoon the cake mixture over the pineapple slices and spread it out evenly using a palette knife. Bake for 40–45 minutes, or until brown on top and a skewer inserted into the centre of the cake comes out clean.

5. Leave to cool in the tin for 5 minutes, then carefully turn onto a serving plate. Remove the tin to reveal the pineapple. Serve with cream or ice cream.

In 1892 Captain John Kidwell, an English horticulturalist, was the first to can pineapple.

most famous are grown in Colebrook, England. Richard Cox, a retired brewer.

STRAWBERRY & BANANA COCONUT CRUMBLE

Crumbles are always welcome on my table, and I'm sure on yours, too! This one has a great combination of strawberries and bananas, and then there's coconut in the crumble topping to make it that little bit different.

Serves 5–6

600g (1lb 5oz) strawberries, hulled

2 bananas

2 tbsp lime juice

pouring cream or custard, to serve

For the crumble topping:

125g (4½oz) unsalted butter

150g (5½oz) plain flour

50g (1¾oz) desiccated coconut

85g (3oz) light muscovado sugar

1. Preheat the oven to 200°C/fan 180°C/gas mark 6. To make the crumble topping, rub the butter into the flour with your fingertips until the mixture resembles breadcrumbs, then stir in the coconut and sugar.

2. Roughly chop the strawberries and peel and slice the bananas. Place the fruit into a 25cm (10in) square ovenproof dish that is at least 7cm (2¾in) deep, add the lime juice and stir to combine. Sprinkle over the crumble topping and bake for 35–40 minutes or until slightly brown on top. Serve with cream or custard.

APPLE PUDDING WITH RUM & RAISIN SYRUP

A fabulous pudding to follow Sunday lunch. It's based on the French batter pudding clafoutis, but has been well and truly dubbed-up!

1. Preheat the oven to 200°C/fan 180°C/gas mark 6. To make the syrup, heat the 400ml (14fl oz) rum, water and sugar in a saucepan over a medium heat. Bring to the boil, stirring occasionally to help the sugar dissolve. Add the raisins and orange rind and boil for 8 minutes or until the raisins have plumped up and the liquid has thickened to a light syrup. Set aside to cool, then add the remaining 4 tbsp rum.

2. Meanwhile, make the batter. Heat the cream and milk in a saucepan set over a medium heat, stirring continuously. Bring almost to the boil. Beat the eggs, sugar and salt together in a large bowl, using an electric mixer or by hand, until the mixture triples in volume and is pale and fluffy. Fold in the flour and orange rind, then stir in the milk mixture and rum.

3. Peel, core and slice the apples, place them in a 1.25-litre (2⅕-pint) shallow gratin dish and sprinkle with the brown sugar. Pour over the batter and bake for 30—40 minutes or until the batter is set and golden.

4. Scatter with the toasted hazelnuts and sift a little icing sugar over the top. Serve warm with the syrup in a jug on the side. Crème fraîche is good with this rather than whipped cream as it needs a bit of tartness.

Serves 6

600g (1lb 5oz) cooking apples
4 tbsp soft light brown sugar
crème fraîche, to serve

For the syrup:
400ml (14fl oz) white or dark
    rum, plus 4 tbsp
200ml (⅓ pint) water
125g (4½oz) granulated sugar
50g (1¾oz) raisins
2 broad strips of unwaxed
    orange rind

For the batter:
150ml (¼ pint) double cream
150ml (¼ pint) milk
3 free-range eggs
125g (4½oz) caster sugar
pinch of salt
40g (1½oz) plain flour
finely grated rind of 1
    unwaxed orange
3 tbsp white or dark rum

To decorate:
1 tbsp roughly chopped
    toasted hazelnuts
icing sugar, for dusting

BAKED APPLES STUFFED WITH HONEYED MANGO & PECANS

This is an easy pud to make for supper and brings some tropical warmth to a dark winter's night.

Serves 6

90g (3¼oz) dried mango

3 tbsp orange juice

90g (3¼oz) pecans, roughly chopped

3 tbsp clear honey

large pinch of cinnamon

¾ tsp finely grated unwaxed orange rind

6 cooking apples

pouring cream or vanilla ice cream, to serve

1. Preheat the oven to 160°C/fan 140°C/gas mark 3. Place the mango in a bowl with the orange juice. Leave to soak for 10 minutes, then cut the mango into small pieces, reserving any remaining juice. Mix the mango and the reserved juice with the pecans, honey, cinnamon and orange rind, and set aside.

2. Core the apples using a small sharp knife or an apple corer, then score a thin line around the outside of each one to help prevent them splitting in the oven.

3. Line a baking sheet with nonstick baking paper, then place the apples on top. Stuff the apples with the honeyed mango and pecan mixture and bake for 50–60 minutes or until the apples are tender (the cooking time will vary according to the type and size of apple). Serve with cream or vanilla ice cream.

Serve warm with cream or ice cream

CHOC-CHIP STEAMIE

I love the look and I love the taste of this. There's nothing more comforting than a steamed pudding and, with chocolate chips in it, it's even better.

Serves 6

175g (6oz) self-raising flour

3 tbsp cocoa powder

pinch of salt

100g (3½oz) unsalted butter, softened, plus extra for greasing

100g (3½oz) light muscovado sugar

2 free-range eggs

2–3 tbsp milk

150g (5½oz) white chocolate chips

To serve:

1 quantity Chocolate Sauce (*see* page 94)

custard or crème fraiche

1. Sift the flour, cocoa powder and salt into a bowl and stir to combine. Beat the butter and sugar together, using an electric mixer or by hand, until pale and fluffy. Add the eggs to the butter and sugar mixture one at a time, alternating with spoonfuls of the dry ingredients, and beat with the mixer set on a low speed or stir gently by hand after each addition. Stir in enough milk to achieve a dropping consistency, then fold in the chocolate chips.

2. Spoon the mixture into a greased 1 litre (1¾ pint) pudding basin and cover with foil. Place an upturned saucer in a large saucepan with a lid and pour in roughly 6cm (2½in) water. Put the pudding basin in the saucepan on top of the saucer and place over a medium heat. Bring the water to the boil, reduce the heat slightly, place the lid on the saucepan and steam for 1½ hours, checking from time to time to ensure the water doesn't boil dry.

3. Drizzle over a little of the Chocolate Sauce and serve with the remaining sauce and custard or crème fraîche on the side.

PASSION FRUIT & ORANGE SOUFFLÉ

I can sure get passionate about this dish – it's so fruity and refreshing, and light as air. Soufflés aren't as hard to make as you'd think, and this one is a true winner.

Serves 6

50g (1¾oz) unsalted butter, plus extra for greasing

50g (1¾oz) caster sugar, plus extra for dusting

50g (1¾oz) plain flour

300ml (½ pint) orange juice

finely grated rind of ½ an unwaxed orange

pulp and seeds of 4 large passion fruit

4 free-range egg whites

icing sugar, for dusting

pouring cream, to serve

1. Preheat the oven to 200°C/fan 180°C/gas mark 6. Grease an 850ml (1½ pint), 15cm (6in) diameter, 6cm (2½in) deep soufflé dish and dust it with caster sugar.

2. Melt the butter in a saucepan set over a low heat and stir in the flour. Cook for a couple of minutes, stirring continuously, then add the orange juice and rind. Simmer for 2 minutes or until the mixture thickens, stirring frequently. Stir in the sugar and passion fruit, then remove from the heat and set aside to cool.

3. Whisk the egg whites until stiff, then fold them into the cooled orange and passion fruit mixture. Pour into the prepared soufflé dish and bake for 20 minutes or until risen. Serve immediately, dusted with icing sugar and accompanied by some cream.

PEAR CAKE WITH CRUNCHY PECAN TOPPING

Toffee-ish and autumnal, this is a great pudding to share.

Serves 8

175g (6oz) unsalted butter,
    softened, plus extra for
    greasing
150g (5½oz) soft light brown
    sugar
2 free-range eggs
225g (8oz) self-raising flour
1 tsp vanilla extract
½ tsp bicarbonate of soda
150ml (¼ pint) soured cream
finely grated rind of 1
    unwaxed lemon
50g (1¾oz) pecans, freshly
    ground
2 large ripe pears
1 tbsp lemon juice
crème fraiche or whipped cream,
    to serve

For the topping:
50g (1¾oz) unsalted butter
50g (1¾oz) soft light brown
    sugar
4 tbsp double cream
85g (3oz) pecans, roughly
    chopped

1. Preheat the oven to 200°C/fan 180°C/gas mark 6 and grease and base-line a 20cm (8in) diameter round loose-bottomed cake tin.

2. Beat the butter and sugar together, using an electric mixer or by hand, until pale and fluffy. Add one of the eggs and beat with the mixer set on a low speed or stir gently by hand to combine. Add a spoonful of the flour and then the remaining egg and beat gently again. Add the vanilla extract, mix to combine, then fold in half of the remaining flour and the bicarbonate of soda. Stir in the soured cream, lemon rind, ground pecans and the remaining flour.

3. Peel, core and slice the pears. Immediately toss them with the lemon juice to stop them going brown. Spoon half the cake mixture into the tin, cover with the pears, then add the remaining cake mixture. Bake for 40 minutes.

4. Meanwhile, make the topping. Melt the butter in a saucepan set over a medium heat, then stir in the sugar, cream and pecans. Heat until the sugar has melted, then remove from the heat and set aside.

5. Remove the cake from the oven and scatter the topping over the top. Return to the oven for a further 20–25 minutes, or until the top is dark gold and a skewer inserted into the centre of the cake comes out clean. Leave the cake to cool in the tin for 15 minutes, then turn out onto a serving plate. Serve with crème fraîche or whipped cream.

Mango & Passion Fruit Dacquoise

Wow, this is easy to make and such a big show-off dessert. It is very good for Christmas when you've had enough of puddings made with dried fruit. If you'd rather not make your own passion-fruit curd, then substitute with ready-made lemon curd and spoon the pulp and juice of five passion fruits over the mango before adding the second layer of meringue.

Serves 8

5 free-range egg whites	For the passion-fruit curd:
large pinch of cream of tartar	6 passion fruit
280g (10oz) caster sugar	85g (3oz) caster sugar
115g (4oz) ground almonds	25g (1oz) unsalted butter
200ml (⅓ pint) double cream	2 free-range eggs, plus 2 yolks,
4 tbsp Greek yogurt	lightly beaten
1 mango	
juice of 1 lime	
icing sugar, for dusting	

1. Preheat the oven to 160°C/fan 140°C/gas mark 3. Line 2 baking sheets with nonstick baking paper and draw a 23cm (9in) diameter circle on each (use a plate to help you).

2. Whisk the egg whites and the cream of tartar together until stiff, then add 3 tbsp caster sugar. Whisk again until the mixture is stiff and shiny, then fold in the remaining sugar and the ground almonds. Spoon the mixture onto the circles on the baking sheets, dividing it equally and spreading it flat.

3. Bake for 1 hour, then remove from the oven and leave to cool on the baking sheets for a few minutes. Peel the paper from the meringues, transfer to wire racks and cool completely.

4. To make the passion-fruit curd, halve the passion fruit and spoon the pulp and seeds into a food processor. Whizz briefly. Put a sieve over a small bowl and push the pulp through it. Keep half the seeds and discard the rest.

5. Put the passion-fruit pulp, sugar, butter, eggs and egg yolks into a bowl set over a saucepan of simmering water, ensuring that the bottom of the bowl doesn't touch the water. Stir continuously with a wooden spoon for 30–40 minutes, or until the mixture has a custard-like consistency and coats the back of the spoon. Remove from the heat, stir in the reserved passion fruit seeds then leave to cool before refrigerating.

6. Whip the cream to soft peaks and fold in the yogurt. Cut the cheeks from the mango, then cut a criss-cross pattern into the flesh of the cheeks without cutting right through the skin. Invert the skin so the flesh stands proud in a pattern of cubes. Run a knife between the flesh and skin to cut the flesh off in neat cubes. Remove the remaining flesh from the skin using a peeler. Squeeze the lime juice over the fruit.

7. Spread one of the meringue circles with the cream mixture. Spoon the passion-fruit curd over the mixture and arrange the mango pieces on top. Place the other meringue circle on top, dust with icing sugar and serve immediately.

RUM BABAS

Makes 10

For the rum syrup:
200g (7oz) caster sugar
300ml (½ pint) water
3 tbsp dark rum

For the babas:
70g (2½oz) unsalted butter,
  melted, plus extra for
  greasing
260g (9½oz) plain flour
25g (1oz) caster sugar
2 × 7g sachets fast-action
  dried yeast
140ml (4½fl oz) warm milk
1 free-range egg, separated,
  plus 1 yolk
finely grated rind of
  1 unwaxed lime
strawberries and pouring
  cream, to serve

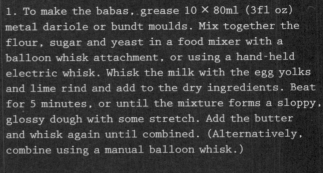

1. To make the babas, grease 10 × 80ml (3fl oz) metal dariole or bundt moulds. Mix together the flour, sugar and yeast in a food mixer with a balloon whisk attachment, or using a hand-held electric whisk. Whisk the milk with the egg yolks and lime rind and add to the dry ingredients. Beat for 5 minutes, or until the mixture forms a sloppy, glossy dough with some stretch. Add the butter and whisk again until combined. (Alternatively, combine using a manual balloon whisk.)

2. Transfer the dough to a bowl and cover with a cloth. Leave to rise in a warm place for 30–60 minutes or until doubled in size. Preheat the oven to 180°C/fan 160°C/gas mark 4.

3. Meanwhile, make the syrup. Heat the sugar and water in a small saucepan over a low heat and simmer gently, stirring occasionally, until the sugar has dissolved. Bring to the boil and boil hard for 3 minutes. Stir in the rum and set aside to cool.

4. Punch down the dough (the mixture will feel sticky) and divide into 10 pieces. Put a piece into each mould and bake for 15 minutes, or until well risen and lightly brown.

5. Leave the babas to cool for 5 minutes, then run a sharp knife around the edge of each mould. Turn the babas out, prick them all over and spoon over the syrup, turning as you do, so each side gets a soaking. Leave for 10 minutes, then repeat. They will soak up the syrup.

6. Serve warm with strawberries and pouring cream, or keep for up to a couple of days in the refrigerator and serve cool.

Use dariole or bundt moulds for the very best result.

BAKED GINGER & CHOCOLATE STUFFED PEARS

Serves 4

50g (1¾oz) ginger biscuits
35g (1¼oz) dark chocolate
35g (1¼oz) hazelnuts,
   roughly chopped
1 small free-range egg
2 tbsp soft light brown sugar
¼ tsp ground cinnamon
1 tbsp cocoa powder
4 slightly under-ripe pears
300ml (½ pint) marsala
50ml (2fl oz) water
25g (1oz) caster sugar
finely grated rind and juice
   of 1 unwaxed orange
½ cinnamon stick
icing sugar, for dusting (optional)

Even under-ripe pears can be given a little *va va voom* with ginger, cinnamon and, of course, chocolate. If you don't have marsala, you can use sweet sherry instead.

1. Preheat the oven to 200°C/ fan 180°C/gas mark 6. Roughly crush the biscuits, chocolate and hazelnuts either in a food processor or by placing them in a sealed bag and bashing with a rolling pin. Mix with the egg, brown sugar, ground cinnamon and cocoa powder.

2. Peel, core and halve the pears and arrange, cut-side up, in an ovenproof dish. Spoon the biscuit mixture into the hollows left by the cores.

3. Heat the marsala with the water, caster sugar, orange rind and juice and the cinnamon stick in a saucepan set over a medium heat, stirring occasionally, until the sugar has dissolved.

4. Pour the liquid around the pears. Bake for 40–45 minutes, or until the pears are soft and the tops are golden. (The cooking time really depends on the ripeness of your pears, so check after 30 minutes. If the tops are beginning to look too dark before the pears are soft, cover them with tin foil.)

5. Serve the pears with the cooking juices, and dust lightly with icing sugar, if liked.

FRESH & FRUITY
Puds

FRUIT COCKTAIL, CARIBBEAN STYLE

Use any summer or tropical fruit in this but don't go wild and use too many – you need to taste them all properly.

Serves 6–8

400g (14oz) strawberries,
  hulled

2 oranges

½ charentais melon

½ gala melon

ginger ice cream, to serve
  (optional)

For the syrup:

100ml (3½fl oz) white rum, plus 4 tbsp

100ml (3½fl oz) orange juice

100ml (3½fl oz) pineapple juice

50ml (2fl oz) water

150g (5½oz) granulated sugar

juice of 3 limes

12 mint leaves

1 tbsp Curaçao

1. To make the syrup, heat the 100ml (3½fl oz) rum, fruit juices, water, sugar and half the lime juice in a saucepan over a medium heat and bring to the boil, stirring occasionally, until the sugar has dissolved. Add 6 of the mint leaves and boil until reduced by half. Add the remaining lime juice, remove from the heat and set aside to cool and thicken. Remove the mint leaves and discard, then add the remaining rum and the Curaçao and chill in the refrigerator.

2. Cut the strawberries into thick slices and place in a serving bowl. Remove the peel and pith from the oranges, break each orange into segments and, using a very sharp knife, cut through the membrane at the top of each segment so that the segment opens out in half like a butterfly. Press the segment open so it stays in that shape and remove any seeds (this is the way my granny used to prepare oranges). Put the orange segments into the serving bowl.

3. Quarter the melons and remove and discard the seeds. Remove the peel, then cut the flesh into slices, then into chunks. Put these into the bowl with the strawberries and oranges and pour over the chilled syrup. Stir in the remainder of the mint leaves and refrigerate for 30 minutes then eat straight away, with ginger ice cream if you like.

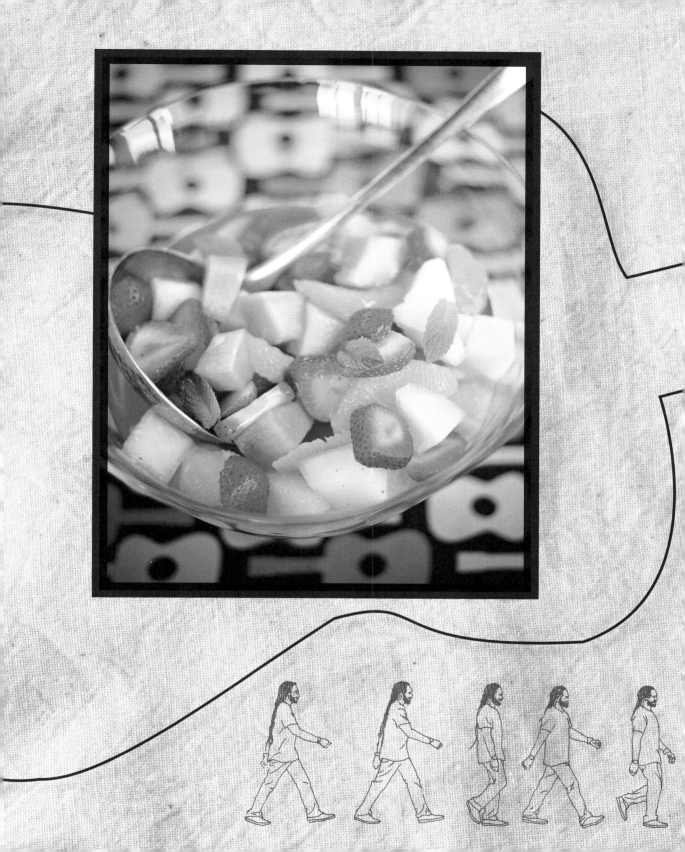

It's hard to believe this pudding is so easy to make – it's literally slice and mix – but when berries are at their best in the height of summer, so why make anything more complicated? This is healthy enough to have for breakfast, but it also makes a lovely pudding.

BERRY PASSION

Serves 4

400g (14oz) strawberries, hulled

4 passion fruit

175g (6oz) blueberries

175g (6oz) raspberries

2 tbsp caster sugar

yogurt, ice cream, pouring cream, whipped cream or crème fraîche, to serve

1. Thickly slice the strawberries and place them in a serving bowl. Halve the passion fruit and scoop the pulp and juice into the bowl. Add the blueberries, raspberries and sugar and gently stir to combine, taking care not to squash the raspberries or bruise the strawberries.

2. Leave to macerate for 15 minutes, then serve with yogurt, ice cream, pouring cream, whipped cream or crème fraîche.

Great with whipped cream 133

ORANGE & CURACAO-SCENTED STRAWBERRIES

If you don't have any Curaçao, or can't get hold of it, then Cointreau, also an orange-flavoured liqueur, will do nicely.

Serves 8

600g (1lb 5oz) strawberries, hulled
75ml (2½fl oz) freshly squeezed orange juice
75ml (2½fl oz) Curaçao
300ml (½ pint) double cream
2 tbsp icing sugar
½ tsp vanilla extract
strips of candied orange rind, to serve (optional)

1. Place the strawberries in a deep bowl, pour over the orange juice and Curaçao, cover with clingfilm and refrigerate for 1 hour, turning them over once or twice.

2. Just before serving, whip the cream to soft peaks and stir in the icing sugar and vanilla extract. Take care not to over-mix — the cream needs to fall in luxurious folds. Serve the strawberries in pretty glasses with a dollop of cream on top. Strips of candied orange rind make a nice finish.

TROPICAL DRIED-FRUIT SALAD

We didn't have much dried fruit when I was growing up in Jamaica because it was always fresh from the tree. But we did have dates, and when you mix them up with other dried fruits and add some lovely stem ginger, you get a fruity pudding that's easy to make at any time of year.

Serves 6–8

500g (1lb) mixed dried fruit (200g/7oz stoned dates, 150g/5½oz mango and 150g/5½oz pineapple makes a good mix)

300ml (½ pint) freshly squeezed orange juice

5 pieces of preserved stem ginger in syrup, plus 3 tbsp syrup

50ml (2fl oz) lime juice

To serve:

8 mint leaves

vanilla, mango or coconut ice cream (optional)

For the rum and honey syrup:

3 tbsp dark rum

750ml (1 pint 3⅓ fl oz) water

250ml (9fl oz) strong Earl Grey tea

2 tbsp clear honey

1. Place the dried fruit in a bowl and pour over the orange juice. Set aside to soak for 20 minutes, in which time the fruit will absorb the juice, then cut the fruit into pieces roughly 3–4cm (1¼–1½in) square.

2. Meanwhile make the rum and honey syrup. Heat the rum, water, tea and honey in a saucepan over a medium heat. Bring to the boil and simmer for 10 minutes. Add the fruit to the saucepan. Bring back to the boil then reduce the heat and simmer gently for 5 minutes, stirring occasionally.

3. Finely slice the stem ginger and add to the pan along with the ginger syrup and lime juice. Stir, remove from the heat and set aside to cool, then cover with clingfilm and refrigerate (this is best left for 2 or 3 days before serving to enable the flavours to develop).

4. To serve, chop the mint leaves and stir them into the fruit salad. This is delicious just on its own, or you can serve it with vanilla, mango or coconut ice cream.

SCENTED FRUIT SALAD

Use whatever fruits are in season or you can get hold of, choosing the most tropical ones. Mangos, pineapples, lychees and papayas are all good, but so are less exotic fruits, such as grapes, melons, oranges and grapefruit. You will need about 800g-1 kg (1lb 12oz-2lb 4oz) of prepared fruit.

Serves 6

1 large mango, peeled, stoned and cubed

½ papaya, peeled, seeds removed, and cubed

1 small pineapple, skin and 'eyes' removed, cored and cut into chunks

14 lychees, peeled and stoned

1 pink grapefruit, peeled and cut into segments

For the syrup:

100g (3½oz) granulated sugar

150ml (¼ pint) water

2 broad strips unwaxed lemon rind

2 cardamom pods

leaves from 1 small bunch of fresh mint

squeeze of lemon juice

3 tbsp orange-flower water, or to taste

1. To make the syrup, heat the sugar, water and lemon rind in a saucepan over a low heat, stirring occasionally, until the sugar has dissolved. Meanwhile bruise the cardamom pods using a pestle and mortar or a rolling pin (don't pulverize them — you want to release some of the scent without destroying the casing) — and add them to the saucepan. Bring to the boil and simmer for 2 minutes. Remove from the heat, add the mint leaves, reserving a few for decoration, and the lemon juice. Cover and set aside to cool.

2. Put the prepared fruit into a glass bowl. Remove the mint leaves from the syrup and discard them. Add the orange-flower water to the syrup and then pour it over the salad (don't go mad with the orange-flower water — the salad should be 'scented', not overpowered!). Decorate the salad with the reserved mint leaves and serve.

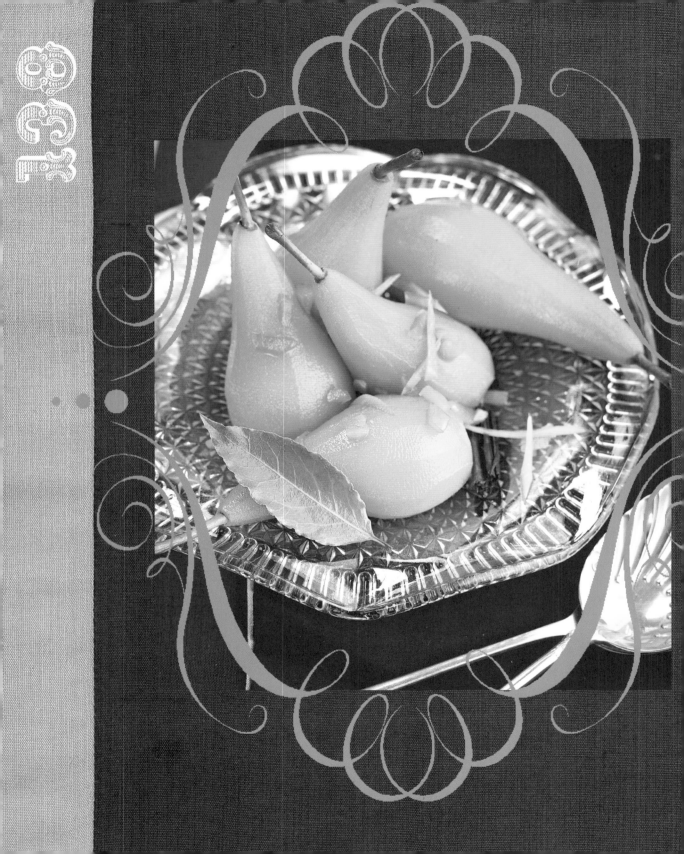

PEARS IN GINGER SYRUP

You can use firm, under-ripe pears for this dish, which combines ginger wine and spices as the base of a delicious syrup. Ginger wine is very Jamaican; I remember it from my youth, and there are lots of reggae songs about Stone's Ginger Wine. If you can find one, sing along as you cook.

Serves 8

300ml (½ pint) ginger wine

300ml (½ pint) water

200g (7oz) soft light brown sugar

2 pieces of preserved stem ginger in syrup, finely chopped

3 thick strips unwaxed lemon rind

2 bay leaves

2 cinnamon sticks, halved

8 firm pears, peeled but stalks retained

double cream, to serve

1. Preheat the oven to 200°C/fan 180°C/gas mark 6. Place all of the ingredients except the pears and cream in a bowl and stir to combine. Arrange the pears in one layer on their sides in a 23cm (9in) square, 6cm (2½in) deep ovenproof dish.

2. Pour the ginger wine mixture over the pears, cover with tin foil and bake for 20 minutes. Remove the foil, carefully turn the pears over and return to the oven for a further 30 minutes, then turn the pears again and bake for a final 10 minutes.

3. Transfer the pears, bay leaves, lemon rind and cinnamon sticks to a serving bowl. Heat the liquid from the ovenproof dish in a saucepan over a medium heat. Bring to the boil and simmer for 10 minutes to reduce, then pour over the pears. Serve with double cream.

139

LEVI'S AMBROSIA

I discovered this dish quite recently. Ambrosia is very popular in the southern states of America, though there it can be quite a kitsch dish – some people even put mini marshmallows in it! If you go the fresh route, which I do, this is a fantastic, healthy pudding. In the States they sprinkle the top with sweetened dried coconut, but I do a little Caribbean trick – one of my favourite snacks as a child was a little bowl of freshly grated coconut with lime juice and demerara sugar. It makes the perfect topping for this.

Serves 8

2 oranges
1 yellow grapefruit
1 pink grapefruit
1 small pineapple
juice of 2 limes
3 tbsp caster sugar, or to taste
8 lime wedges, to decorate

For the topping:
flesh from ½ coconut, grated
juice of 1–2 limes
3 tbsp demerara sugar

1. Slice the ends from each of the citrus fruits then cut away the skin and pith using a small sharp knife. Slice the fruit, removing the seeds, and place in a serving bowl.

2. Cut the top and bottom off the pineapple and cut away the skin. Remove the 'eyes' and slice the pineapple into quarters lengthways. Remove the hard core from each quarter, then cut each quarter into slices widthways and place the slices in the serving bowl with the citrus fruits.

3. Add the lime juice and sugar to the bowl and stir to combine, taking care not to break up the fruit. Refrigerate to macerate for 1–6 hours until ready to serve.

4. To serve, sprinkle over the coconut, lime juice and sugar and decorate with lime wedges. Enjoy the taste of sunshine!

KUMQUATS WITH LIME & WHITE RUM

You don't see kumquats very often, but snap them up if you do - they make a lovely grown-up bitter-sweet compote to eat with ice cream. A good stem-ginger ice cream - see page 171 for mine - is knock-out.

Serves 6

400g (14oz) kumquats
250g (9oz) caster sugar
250ml (9fl oz) water
rind and juice of 2 unwaxed
    limes (rind removed in strips)
2 tbsp white rum, or to taste

1. Remove the stalks from the kumquats and quarter the fruit, removing any pips. Place them in a saucepan over a medium heat with the sugar, water, lime rind and half the lime juice. Bring to the boil then simmer, stirring occasionally, until the sugar has dissolved.

2. Reduce the heat and cook, uncovered, for 20—30 minutes, or until the kumquats are soft and the juices are syrupy, stirring occasionally. Pour into a serving bowl and allow to cool. Add the remaining lime juice and the rum, and serve.

BANANA CINNAMON TOAST

Cinnamon is one of my favourite spices and this sweet snack is a terrific tea-time treat – yet another great way to enjoy bananas.

Serves 4

1 banana
4 thick slices white bread
unsalted butter, for spreading
2 tbsp caster sugar
½ tsp ground cinnamon
lime wedges, to decorate

1. Preheat the grill to medium. Peel the banana and cut it into 2cm (¾in) slices. Toast the bread on one side under the grill. Spread the untoasted sides with a generous amount of butter and top with the banana slices. Sprinkle over the caster sugar and cinnamon.

2. Return the toast to the grill and cook until the sugar is melted and golden. Leave to cool slightly. (If you like, you can squish down the banana a bit to spread over the toast.) Cut each piece of toast into 4 triangles. Decorate with lime wedges and serve.

FRENCH TOAST WITH GRIDDLED MANGO CHEEKS & LIME SYRUP

Eggy bread given the Caribbean treatment! This is a brilliant dish for a weekend brunch. If you get your syrup and mangos prepared in advance you just have to cook the bread at the last minute.

Serves 4

2 mangos
150ml (¼ pint) double cream
2 free-range eggs, plus 1 yolk
2 tbsp caster sugar
8 slices brioche
50g (1¾oz) unsalted butter

For the lime syrup:
150ml (¼ pint) water
150g (5½oz) granulated sugar
finely grated rind and juice
   of 2 unwaxed limes

1. To make the lime syrup, heat the water, sugar and lime juice in a saucepan over a medium heat, stirring occasionally. Bring to the boil and simmer for 10 minutes, then remove from the heat and set aside for 40 minutes. Add the lime rind and chill in the refrigerator.

2. Peel the mangos and cut the cheeks neatly from each side of the stone. Cut this flesh into crescent-shaped slices and set aside.

3. Whisk the cream, eggs, egg yolk and sugar together in a bowl. Cut the brioche slices in half diagonally and place 4 pieces into the egg mixture for about a minute. Meanwhile, melt a knob of the butter in a nonstick frying pan, then cook the eggy brioche until golden on each side and transfer to a piece of kitchen paper. Dunk the next 4 slices of bread in the egg mixture and repeat until all of the slices are cooked.

4. Heat a griddle pan over a high heat and cook the mango slices on either side until charred stripes form. The mangos don't have to cook through — this is really for appearance only.

5. Divide the brioche slices between 4 plates and top with the mango slices. Pour over the lime syrup and serve.

144

BANANA PANCAKES

Breakfast and brunch are so much better with pancakes on the table, and this recipe brings something a bit different to the gathering.

Serves 3-4

100g (3½oz) plain flour
1 tsp baking powder
pinch of salt
1 tbsp light muscovado sugar
½ tsp ground cinnamon
grated nutmeg, to taste
1 ripe banana
175ml (6fl oz) milk
1 free-range egg, beaten
unsalted butter, for frying

To serve:
maple syrup
2 bananas, peeled and thinly
   sliced

1. Mix the flour, baking powder, salt, sugar and spices together in a bowl. Mash the banana and place in a jug. Pour over the milk, add the egg and whisk to combine. Make a well in the centre of the dry ingredients and pour in the milk mixture. Whisk the dry ingredients into the wet until the mixture has the consistency of double cream.

2. Melt a little butter in a frying pan. Put tablespoons of the batter into the pan and fry on both sides, turning when small holes appear on the top of the pancakes.

3. Serve the pancakes drizzled with maple syrup, adding extra thinly sliced bananas on top.

146

148

CHILLI PINEAPPLE

This is one of the easiest and yet most delicious ways to enjoy a sweet, juicy pineapple, made even sweeter and juicier by the simple addition of some chilli.

SERVES 4

1 ripe and juicy pineapple | 2 limes | 1–2 tsp chilli powder, or to taste

1. Cut the top and bottom off the pineapple and use a sharp knife to cut away the peel and 'eyes'. Quarter the pineapple lengthways and cut the hard core from each quarter. Cut each quarter into thick slices lengthways.

2. Arrange the pineapple slices on a large platter for people to help themselves, or divide between 4 serving plates. Squeeze over the juice of 1 of the limes and slice the other into wedges. Add the lime wedges to the platter or plates.

3. Just before serving, sprinkle over the chilli powder (do this from a height to disperse the chilli evenly). You can always squeeze over some more lime and dip the pineapple in more chilli powder, if you like.

ELDERFLOWER JELLY TRIFLE

I love the subtle, delicate flavour of elderflower, and this mouth-watering, fruity trifle really shows it off! Elderflower cordial varies in strength, so be careful not to add too much.

Serves 6

For the jelly:
8 small leaves gelatine (weighing 13 g in total)
600ml (1 pint) water
75ml (2½fl oz) elderflower cordial, or to taste
2 tbsp caster sugar
175g (6oz) mango flesh, cut into small chunks
140g (5oz) hulled strawberries, cut into small chunks
125g (4½oz) blueberries

For the sponge:
3 tsp elderflower cordial
100g (3½oz) ready-made Madeira cake, cut into small pieces

For the elderflower cream:
100ml (3½fl oz) whipping cream
1–2 tsp elderflower cordial

1. To make the jelly, place the gelatine leaves in a bowl and pour over half of the water. Leave to soak for 5 minutes. Meanwhile, heat the remaining water with the elderflower cordial and sugar in a small saucepan over a low heat, stirring occasionally until the sugar has dissolved. Remove from the heat, pour the gelatine and its soaking liquid into the pan and stir until the leaves dissolve. Set aside to cool.

2. To prepare the sponge layer, sprinkle a little of the elderflower cordial around the bottom of 6 large wine glasses or tumblers and top with the pieces of Madeira cake. Sprinkle the remaining elderflower cordial over the cake.

3. Divide the fruit evenly among the glasses, pushing it down into the sponge slightly. Carefully pour over the jelly mixture, ensuring the sponge doesn't float up (it should be weighed down by the fruit). Chill the glasses in the refrigerator until the jelly is set, or overnight.

4. For the elderflower cream, whisk the cream into soft peaks and stir in the elderflower cordial. Spoon the cream over the jelly and serve immediately.

150

BARBECUED

Puds

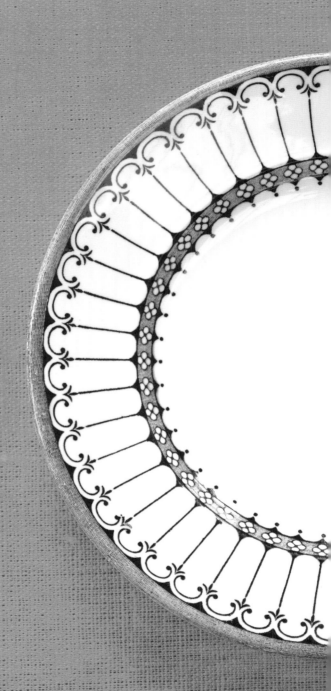

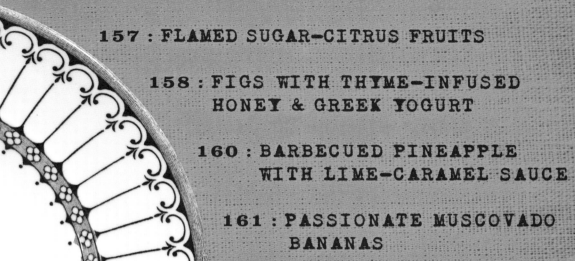

Bananas n
which hastens
placed next to

n tell   national
k. Others   elegant

a point. But ... ets have always insisted tha
way to really ... country and its people is to
eating habits ... food they eat, the way they
their attitude ... ds and eating habits alien to

Though ... above is doubtless a little e
the food theor... erhaps the one that will sta
under examin... the case of our country, f
we all know ... is a very colourful place
contrast... ve know it is a lusty cou
times to ... t blessed with a ce
elegan... country very eager to
with ... ng pattern for living
some... eigner. And we kno
all ... re strongly reflected
we ... re it, not to mention
to f... ... to us.

... examples: Why is the
esta... od in Jamaica a salted fish fo
wate... be imported at great expens
we concen... ch on starches instead of loo
for proteins a... m meat, which is admittedl
for our low-in... roups? Why do we concentra
paratively few... which, although certainly de
to grow mon... in a lifetime of eating? W
eat more gree... s?

The ans... these questions lie, of cou

BUNCH OF BANANAS

BANANAS, 1.

Arms of Mauritius

Important Industries of the British Empire

MAURITIUS : SUGAR

Mauritius is the biggest producer of sugar within the British Colonial Empire, and for the year beginning 1st September, 1938, the amount available for distribution from the island (under the International Sugar Agreement) was 252,000 tons. The sugar cane grows to an average height of 12 feet, and new canes take about 18 to 20 months to attain maturity. Our picture shows the ripe canes being cut and loaded for transport to the factory, where the juice is extracted by crushing.

Typhoo Series of 25   No.

PONY EXPRESS
BRAND
PITTED
RED CHERRIES

GARETTES.

CANARY IS

DIES

ATLANTIC
OCEAN

A

ANAS
LY GROWN.

BANANAS.

reetings
from
amaica"

CUTTING

H. K. & F. B. THURBER & CO.
NEW YORK.
CALIFORNIA
BARTLETT PEAR

CALIFORNIA APRICOTS
H. K. & F. B.
THURBER & CO.
New York.

re lu
o produce ca
virtual
and Ac
But w
s, coco
to pre

ral differe
and ideas

sting dish
ge but is v
sing Jerke
ies; a new

(gr
pea
exce

to l
Pin
mu
wit
Jan
Pur
sam

glos
and many wonderful drinks, both alcoholic and
The alcoholic drinks are all new, with the exce
Rum Sour and the Rum Punch which is incl
nowadays it seems almost impossible to get a go
mixed in a private home.

The magazine does not pretend to be all-co
But the Jamaica Information Service has iss
hope that it will stimulate a new way of think
Jamaica. It is hoped, too, that this new way o

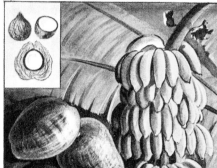

UITHEEMSE FRUITSOORTEN
1. DE BANAAN - DE COCOSNOOT
OXO BOUILLON : rijk aan vleesextract
Nadruk verboden   Verklaring op keerzijde

156

FLAMED SUGAR-CITRUS FRUITS

You need to cook these over a flaming barbecue at the start of the cooking and before you cook any meat. Cool, then devour!

Serves 8

2 large oranges

1 pink grapefruit

1 yellow grapefruit

6 tbsp soft light brown sugar

1 tbsp finely chopped rosemary

2 tsp ground allspice

1. Cut the oranges and grapefruits into quarters, removing the pips. Place the sugar, rosemary and allspice on a large flat plate and use your fingers to combine.

2. Dip the orange and grapefruit quarters into the sugar mixture, coating the flesh sides well and tapping off any excess.

3. Fire up your barbecue and, as it flames, put the sugar-crusted citrus fruits onto the grill (you want to get them right over the flames to help the sugar to caramelize). Cook until the sugar starts to brown (this only takes a couple of minutes), then turn them over.

4. Pile up the fruits on a serving plate and leave to one side as you cook the rest of the food, then serve for pudding, all sweet, charred and juicy.

I love beautiful purple figs with their luscious insides and this is an easy and different way to end a barbecue.

Serves 8

6 tbsp clear honey
2 tsp thyme leaves
16 figs
8 tbsp Greek yogurt

1. Heat the honey and thyme leaves in a small saucepan set over a low heat. When runny, set aside to allow the flavours to infuse.
2. When you've eaten your main course, but the barbecue is still hot, put the whole figs on the grill, turning them over after a minute or so. You want to get them warm rather than charred.
3. Remove the figs from the grill and cut into each, but not all the way through, so they open up into quarters. Put 2 onto each plate. Add a tablespoon of Greek yogurt to each, drizzle over the scented honey and serve immediately.

FIGS WITH THYME~INFUSEL

161

HONEY & GREEK YOGURT

BARBECUED PINEAPPLE WITH LIME-CARAMEL SAUCE

Serves 6

1 large ripe pineapple
vanilla ice cream, to serve

For the lime-caramel sauce:
75ml (2½fl oz) water
150g (5½oz) caster sugar
300ml (½ pint) double cream
85g (3oz) unsalted butter
juice of 2 limes

SOPHISTICATED!

1. For the lime-caramel sauce, heat the water and sugar in a saucepan set over a medium heat. Bring to the boil and simmer, without stirring, until the syrup turns a dark caramel colour. Stir in half the cream using a wooden spoon — stand back as the cream will spit as it hits the caramel. Remove the pan from the heat, add the remaining cream and stir until smooth. Add the butter and lime juice and stir until well combined.

2. Cut the top and bottom off the pineapple and use a sharp knife to cut away the skin and 'eyes'. Halve the pineapple lengthways, then cut each half into 3 wedges. Slice the hard bit of core from each wedge, being careful not to remove too much — the pineapple needs to stay intact while it is barbecued. Grill the wedges on a medium-hot barbecue for about 4 minutes on each side, or until the flesh is singed but still juicy. Serve immediately with vanilla ice cream and the lime-caramel sauce.

160

Passionate
Muscovado Bananas

Serves 6

6 bananas
pinch of ground cinnamon
6 tsp dark muscovado sugar
2 ripe passion fruit
6 Flake chocolate bars
pouring cream, to serve
  (optional)

1. Slice down the length of each banana, going through the skin and most of the flesh but not slicing all the way through. Ease the bananas open. Mix the cinnamon with the sugar and sprinkle the mixture down the centre of each banana.

2. Halve the passion fruit and spoon the pulp into the centre of each banana. Break the chocolate into pieces and wedge some into each banana. Wrap the bananas individually in tin foil and place in the embers of the barbecue. Cook for at least 30 minutes, or until you are ready to eat them. Serve the bananas with cream, if liked.

BANANA SKINS PROTECT THE FRUIT FROM THE COALS

FIRE-ROASTED PEACHES

Peaches taste amazing in this dish, but you can use nectarines, if you prefer, or even plums, although they will take less time to cook. A drop of rum in the parcels doesn't go amiss, should you fancy that, too! Use the cooking times here as guidelines – it depends on the size and ripeness of your fruit, so do check them before the end of the suggested cooking time.

Serves 6

6 just-ripe peaches,
    halved and stoned
35g (1¼oz) unsalted butter
3 tsp vanilla extract
¼ tsp ground cinnamon
3 tbsp granulated sugar

To serve:
flaked almonds, toasted
crème fraîche or vanilla
    ice cream

1. Cut 2 × 45cm (17¾in) squares each of foil and nonstick baking paper. Place the paper on top of the foil. Place the peaches, cut-side up, onto each square (6 halves on each). Dot with the butter and sprinkle over the vanilla extract, cinnamon and sugar. Fold the paper over the peaches, then crimp the foil together to make parcels (they need to be sealed well as you want to keep all the butter and juices inside the parcels when they cook).

2. Put the peach parcels onto the barbecue over medium-hot coals. Cook for about 20 minutes or until soft. (It's hard to go wrong with this dish — your peaches will just get softer the longer you cook them.) Sprinkle with toasted almond flakes and serve with crème fraîche or vanilla ice cream.

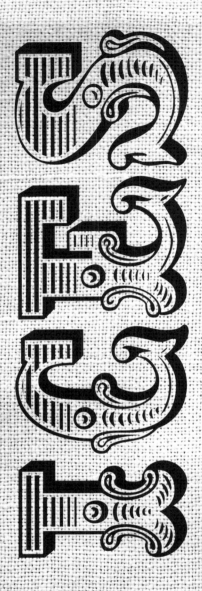

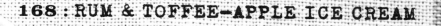

RUM & TOFFEE-APPLE ICE CREAM

The fabulousness of toffee apples in an ice cream! Be careful not to over whip the cream – it should only just hold its shape.

Serves 8

450g (1lb) eating apples
75ml (2½fl oz) water
juice of ½ lemon
125g (4½oz) caster sugar
500ml (18fl oz) whipping cream
5 tbsp white rum

For the caramel:
2 tbsp water
125g (4½oz) granulated sugar
unsalted butter, for greasing

1. To make the caramel, heat the water and sugar in a saucepan set over a medium heat. Bring to the boil and simmer, without stirring, until the syrup turns a dark caramel colour. Pour the caramel immediately in a thin layer onto a buttered baking sheet. Leave to cool, then break the caramel into little shards.

2. Peel, core and slice the apples. Heat in a saucepan with the water and lemon juice over a medium heat until the apples are soft and the water has reduced completely. (Ensure the apples don't burn and add a little more water if needed.) Set aside to cool.

3. Mix the apples with the sugar to form a purée. Whisk the cream until it just holds it shape and fold in the apple purée and rum.

4. Churn the cream in an ice-cream machine according to the manufacturer's instructions. (Alternatively, pour the mixture into a plastic container with a lid and freeze for 3 hours, then remove and whizz in a food processor or beat using an electric mixer, or by hand, to break up the ice crystals. Return to the freezer for 2 hours, whizz or beat again, then return to the freezer for another couple of hours.)

5. When the ice cream is nearly ready, add the caramel chunks or stir them in by hand.

STEM-GINGER ICE CREAM WITH HOT CHOCOLATE SAUCE

I love explosions of flavour, and ginger is one explosive ingredient! This ice cream goes well with pears poached with ginger, if you really want to go to town and ginger up your life. You don't really need the chocolate sauce but it is, so to speak, the icing on the cake.

Serves 6–8

300ml (½ pint) double cream

300ml (½ pint) milk

6 free-range egg yolks

60g (2¼oz) light muscovado sugar

5 pieces of preserved stem ginger in syrup, plus extra, cut into slivers, to decorate, plus 3 tbsp syrup

For the chocolate sauce:

100g (3½oz) dark chocolate, broken into pieces

100ml (3½fl oz) double or whipping cream

1. Heat the cream and milk in a saucepan set over a medium heat until hot but not boiling. Meanwhile, whisk together the egg yolks and sugar. Finely slice the stem ginger and add to the egg mixture along with the ginger syrup.

2. Pour the egg mixture into the pan with the warm milk and cream and cook over a very low heat for 5–10 minutes, or until the mixture coats the back of a spoon, stirring continuously. Leave to cool, then chill in the refrigerator for at least 30 minutes.

3. Churn the cream in an ice-cream machine according to the manufacturer's instructions. (Alternatively, pour the mixture into a plastic container with a lid and freeze for 3 hours, then remove and whizz in a food processor or beat using an electric mixer, or by hand, to break up the ice crystals. Return to the freezer for 2 hours, whizz or beat again, then return to the freezer for another couple of hours.)

4. To make the chocolate sauce, melt the chocolate with the cream in a bowl set above a saucepan of simmering water, ensuring that the base of the bowl doesn't touch the water, stirring occasionally.

5. Remove the ice cream from the freezer 10 minutes before eating. Decorate with slivers of stem ginger and serve with chocolate sauce.

WALK THE PLANK ICE CREAM

You are walking the plank with this ice cream because it's so intensely chocolately, and then you put extra chocolate, cream and rum on top!

Serves 6–8

For the chocolate ice cream:
200g (7oz) dark chocolate, broken into pieces
300ml (½ pint) double cream
300ml (½ pint) milk
2 tbsp cocoa powder
1 free-range egg, plus 1 yolk
50g (1¾oz) dark muscovado sugar
½ tsp vanilla extract
seeds from 5 cardamom pods, crushed

For the rum cream:
200ml (⅓ pint) double cream
1–2 tbsp dark rum, or to taste

For the topping:
2 Flake chocolate bars
white chocolate buttons
chocolate sprinkles

1. To make the chocolate ice cream, put the chocolate in a saucepan with the cream and milk. Heat gently, stirring occasionally, until the chocolate has melted. Do not allow it to boil. Stir in the cocoa powder and set aside to cool slightly.

2. Meanwhile, whisk the egg and egg yolk with the sugar. Pour the cooled cream and chocolate into the mixture and whisk well to combine. Return the mixture to the saucepan and cook over a low heat, stirring continuously, to make a custard. (Do not allow the mixture to overheat or it will turn into scrambled eggs!) If it starts to curdle, whisk hard and strain to remove any lumps.

3. Remove from the heat and add the vanilla extract and cardamom seeds. Leave to cool, then chill in the refrigerator.

4. Churn the cream in an ice-cream machine according to the manufacturer's instructions. (Alternatively, pour the mixture into a plastic container with a lid and freeze for 3 hours, then remove and whizz in a food processor or beat using an electric mixer, or by hand, to break up the ice crystals. Return to the freezer for 2 hours, whizz or beat again, then return to the freezer for another couple of hours.) Transfer to the refrigerator 20 minutes before serving.

5. To make the rum cream, whisk the cream to soft peaks and fold in the rum. To assemble, put scoops of the ice cream in bowls, top with the rum cream and decorate with the Flake, chocolate buttons and chocolate sprinkles.

AFFOGATO, JAMAICAN STYLE

Serves 4

4–8 scoops vanilla ice cream
very strong freshly-brewed
  coffee, to taste
Tia Maria, to taste

Sorry, I can't leave this just to the Italians. It's the best lazy pudding in the world!

Put a scoop (or 2) of vanilla ice cream into 4 heatproof glasses or cups. Immediately pour over the coffee, add the Tia Maria and, before the ice cream can melt, quickly serve. It's best to be standing by as people will definitely want seconds…

PASSION FRUIT & ORANGE SORBET

This really tastes of passion fruit but, because the orange juice gives so much flavour, you don't have to use that many of them – I always remember that passion fruit are expensive! This dish is so good, I just serve it on its own or with a couple of fancy biscuits.

Serves 8

140g (5oz) granulated sugar

425ml (¾ pint) water

finely grated rind and juice of 1 unwaxed lemon

10 passion fruit

approximately 150ml (¼ pint) freshly squeezed orange juice

1 free-range egg white

cigarette russe biscuits, to serve (optional)

1. Put the sugar in a saucepan and pour over the water. Heat gently, stirring frequently, until the sugar has dissolved. Add the lemon rind, increase the heat to medium-high, and bring to the boil. Boil for 5 minutes, uncovered, or until reduced to a syrup. Set aside to cool completely.

2. Halve the passion fruit and scoop the pulp into a nylon sieve set over a measuring jug. Push the juice and pulp through the sieve, discard half the seeds and add the rest to the jug. Pour in enough orange juice to make the liquid up to 300ml (½ pint). Pour in the cooled sugar syrup and the lemon juice and chill in the refrigerator for at least 30 minutes.

3. Beat the egg white in a bowl with a fork until frothy, then stir into the passion fruit syrup. Churn in an ice-cream machine according to the manufacturer's instructions. (Alternatively, pour the mixture into a freezerproof container with a lid and freeze for 2–3 hours, then break up the ice crystals using a fork; repeat 3–4 times, until frozen and smooth.)

4. Take the sorbet out of the freezer shortly before serving to soften. Serve on small plates with some cigarette russe biscuits, if you like.

MANGO & LIME ICE CREAM

Mango needs a little bit of acid to liven it up, so both the lime and the yogurt in this recipe perform an important job. Serve with sliced tropical fruits or drizzled with the lime syrup on page 144.

Serves 8

100g (3½oz) granulated sugar
150ml (¼ pint) water
3 large, really ripe, mangos
juice of 5 limes
200ml (⅓ pint) double cream
6 tbsp Greek yogurt
4 tbsp icing sugar

1. Heat the sugar and water in a saucepan set over a low heat, stirring occasionally, until the sugar has dissolved. Increase the heat, bringing the liquid to the boil, then reduce the heat and simmer gently for 10 minutes or until syrupy. Remove from the heat and set aside to cool.

2. Peel and stone the mangos and place the flesh in a food processor. Whizz into a smooth purée. Transfer to a bowl, add the lime juice and sugar syrup and mix to combine.

3. Whip the cream into soft peaks, then add to the mango and syrup mixture, stirring well to combine. Add the yogurt and icing sugar and beat well to ensure there are no lumps.

4. Churn the cream in an ice-cream machine according to the manufacturer's instructions. (Alternatively, pour the mixture into a plastic container with a lid and place into the coldest part of the freezer for about 2 hours or until it is beginning to freeze around the edges, then remove and beat the frozen edges into the centre using an electric mixer, or by hand. Return to the freezer for 2–3 hours, beat again, then return to the freezer until frozen.) Remove the ice cream from the freezer before serving to soften.

PINEAPPLE & ROSEWATER SORBET

This is one of those dishes that makes you go back to the freezer to get some more… and then some more… and then there's nothing left! I always finish my bowl like a good boy and, with this ice, it's nice. Pineapple and rosewater is one of those magical combinations. Try it – you'll see.

Serves 6–8

500g (1lb 2oz) fresh pineapple
   or 2 × 435g cans pineapple
   chunks, drained
3 tsp rosewater, or to taste

For the sugar syrup:
200g (7oz) granulated sugar
400ml (14fl oz) water
finely grated rind and juice of
   1 unwaxed lemon

1. To make the sugar syrup, heat the sugar and water in a heavy-based saucepan over a low heat, stirring occasionally, until the sugar has dissolved. Bring to the boil and boil rapidly for 3 minutes. Remove from the heat, stir in the lemon rind and juice and set aside to cool.

2. Whizz the cooled syrup and pineapple in a food processor to make a purée. Add the rosewater to taste, remembering that the mixture will taste milder once it is frozen. Churn in an ice-cream machine according to the manufacturer's instructions. (Alternatively, pour the mixture into a plastic container with a lid and freeze for 2–3 hours, then break up the ice crystals using a fork. Repeat 3–4 times until frozen and smooth.)

3. Take the sorbet out of the freezer shortly before serving to soften. Serve this elegant ice in little glass bowls.

PINEAPPLE & RUM GRANITA

A bit of a cheat, this recipe, as I buy the pineapple juice. But it makes a very easy and seriously cooling pud after a hot barbecue.

Serves 8

600ml (1 pint) pineapple juice
100g (3½oz) caster sugar
finely grated rind and juice of
   3 unwaxed limes
5 tbsp white rum

1. Gently heat the pineapple juice with the sugar and most of the lime rind in a saucepan over a low heat, stirring occasionally, until the sugar has dissolved. Set aside to cool completely.

2. Mix the lime juice and rum together in a bowl. Add the pineapple mixture and stir to combine. Pour into a shallow container and freeze for 24 hours (this granita takes longer to freeze than most ices due to the alcohol content), breaking up the ice crystals using a fork 4 or 5 times during the freezing process.

3. Remove from the freezer just before serving as this granita melts quickly due to the high alcohol content.

4. Serve in pretty glass bowls decorated with the remaining grated lime rind.

BANANA & LIME ICED PUDS

An unusual and healthy dessert. This is a good one for kids.
It's also scrumptious as a weekend breakfast. You can get bags
of sweetened shaved coconut in health-food shops.

Serves 6–8

2 large bananas, peeled and
   chopped

300g (10½oz) pineapple, cubed

50ml (2fl oz) double cream

200g (7oz) Greek yogurt

200g (7oz) coconut cream

125g (4½oz) icing sugar

100g (3½oz) desiccated coconut

finely grated rind of 2 unwaxed
   limes and juice of 1, plus extra
   finely grated rind to serve

25–50ml (¾–2fl oz) milk

sweetened coconut shavings,
   to serve

1. Place all the ingredients, except the milk and coconut shavings, in a bowl and stir to combine. Add half the milk and judge the texture before adding more if needed: it will firm up as it chills in the refrigerator, but it shouldn't be too sloppy at this stage.

2. Spoon the mixture into individual glasses and chill in the coldest part of the refrigerator for 1½ hours or until set, then transfer the glasses to the freezer for 15 minutes. (You don't want to freeze the puds, just completely chill them and make them a little firmer. This will also frost the glasses nicely.) Top each serving with a little shaved coconut and lime rind.

STRAWBERRY & HONEY-PINEAPPLE FRUIT LOLLIES

These are so pretty, they appeal to both kids and adults. Have them ready in the freezer for those hot summer days when you want something cool and fruity.

Makes 6

200g (7oz) strawberries, hulled

2–3 tbsp caster sugar, or to taste

½ tsp vanilla extract

½ × 435g can pineapple, in juice

1 tbsp lime juice

2 tbsp clear honey

1. Whizz the strawberries in a liquidizer with the sugar and vanilla extract. Pour into a plastic container with a lid and freeze for 30-60 minutes, or until semi-frozen.

2. Drain the pineapple, reserving the juice. Wash and dry the liquidizer bowl and whizz together the pineapple, 6 tablespoons of the pineapple juice, the lime juice and honey.

3. Spoon the semi-frozen strawberry mixture into 6 ice-lolly moulds, pressing the mixture down with a teaspoon. Top with the pineapple mixture. Press the sticks into the mixture, then freeze the lollies in the freezer until hard.

4. To serve, dip each of the moulds briefly in hot water, then carefully remove the lollies.

TEXTILE.MAHAL.HA

190 : SPICED CHOCOLATE-DIPPED FRUITS

193 : CHOCOLATE FLATTIES

194 : TAMARIND BALLS

196 : RUM & RAISIN FUDGE

198 : BUTTER MAPLE POPCORN

201 : APPLE CRISPS

201 : COCONUT DROPS

189

SPICED CHOCOLATE-DIPPED FRUITS

This is a summery, cricket-watching kind of treat. You can add the spices to the chocolate or, alternatively, buy ready-spiced bars – look out for chilli dark chocolate, cardamom milk chocolate and white chocolate with vanilla.

Serves 8

1 just-ripe mango
1 large seedless orange
8 large strawberries, stems left on

For the spiced chocolate:
85g (3oz) dark chocolate,
   broken into pieces
85g (3oz) milk chocolate,
   broken into pieces
85g (3oz) white chocolate,
   broken into pieces
pinch of ground dried chilli
seeds from 2–3 cardamom pods,
   crushed
seeds from 1 vanilla pod

1. Line a baking sheet with nonstick baking paper. Melt the chocolates separately in bowls set over saucepans of simmering water, stirring occasionally, ensuring that the bases of the bowls don't touch the water. Mix the chilli into the dark chocolate, the cardamom seeds into the milk chocolate and the vanilla seeds into the white chocolate. Set aside to cool slightly.

2. Peel and stone the mango and slice the cheeks into 8 pieces. Peel and segment the orange.

3. Dip half of each piece of fruit into one of the chocolates. Place the chocolate fruit pieces on the lined baking sheet and chill in the refrigerator to set (you can smooth out the chocolate if it is bumpy using a knife dipped briefly in hot water). If the chocolate begins to set before you have dipped all of the fruit, replace the bowl over the saucepan of simmering water to remelt.

CHOCOLATE FLATTIES

These look as pretty as butterfly wings! Bring them to the table to accompany coffee or tea for the perfect end to a meal. The choice of dried fruits and nuts is up to you – this is just what I like.

Makes 20

50g (1¾oz) dark chocolate, broken into pieces

50g (1¾oz) white chocolate, broken into pieces

20 pistachio nuts

20 pecan nuts

20 small pieces of dried mango

20 small pieces of dried pineapple

1 piece of preserved stem ginger in syrup, cut into slivers

1. Line 2 baking sheets with nonstick baking paper. Melt the chocolates separately in bowls set over saucepans of simmering water, stirring occasionally, ensuring that the bases of the bowls don't touch the water. Drop 10 teaspoons of the melted dark chocolate onto a lined baking sheet, and 10 teaspoons of the melted white chocolate onto the other, spreading the chocolate into thin circles approximately 5cm (2in) in diameter.

2. Carefully place 1 pistachio, 1 pecan, and 1 piece each of mango and pineapple onto each chocolate disc, then top with a ginger sliver. Chill in the refrigerator to set, then store them there in a covered container. Serve whenever you fancy a nice piece of homemade 'fruit 'n' nut' chocolate.

194

TAMARIND BALLS

These were one of my favourite sweets when I was a kid.
Sometimes the sugary tamarind paste was formed into
a ball around one of the tamarind seeds and you would suck
it until the seed shone like daylight. I still love tamarind
balls today – they're such natural sweets and have a
lip-smacking sour edge to them.

Makes 12

225g (8oz) tamarinds,
   or enough to make
   85g (3oz) paste

40g (1½oz) granulated sugar
   (or half the weight of the
   tamarind pulp), plus extra
   for rolling

1. Shell the tamarinds and pull the sticky flesh away from the fibres and the seeds (you should have around 85g/3oz of flesh). This is gooey work, but worth it. Finely chop the flesh to make a rough paste.

2. Put the tamarind paste into a bowl with the sugar and knead together well. Divide the mixture into 12 small pieces and roll each piece into a small ball.

3. Sprinkle a plate with sugar and roll each ball in the sugar to lightly coat. Place each ball in a paper sweet case to serve. These keep well in an airtight container.

RUM & RAISIN FUDGE

Fudge is a favourite in Jamaica. The Fudge Man – he's called Fudgie – rides around on a moped and has a little horn that he sounds so everyone comes running.

Makes about 36 pieces

85g (3oz) raisins
4 tbsp dark rum
397g (14oz) granulated sugar
400g can condensed milk
100ml (3½fl oz) water
60g (2¼oz) unsalted butter, plus extra for greasing
2 tsp vanilla extract

1. Place the raisins and rum in a bowl. Set aside to soak for 20 minutes, in which time the fruit will absorb the juice.

2. Meanwhile, heat the sugar, condensed milk and water in a large, heavy-based saucepan over a low heat, stirring occasionally, until the sugar has dissolved. Increase the heat and bring to the boil. (The mixture will froth up like a hot sugar volcano so you need to make sure your pan is big enough!) Stir occasionally to begin with but, after a few minutes, stir frequently to ensure the mixture does not burn. When the mixture reaches 'soft ball' stage, or 118°C (245°F) on a sugar thermometer, remove it from the heat and set it aside to cool slightly. Meanwhile, grease and line a 20 × 20cm (8 × 8in) baking sheet.

3. Stir the vanilla extract and butter into the fudge mixture. Beat vigorously – as the fudge cools, it will thicken and become grainy. You can hurry this process along by placing the pan in a roasting tin half-filled with cool water.) Once the fudge is thick, stir in the rum-soaked raisins. Pour the mixture into the tin and leave to cool.

4. Use a knife to cut the fudge into pieces and serve. These keep well in an airtight container.

We made popcorn a lot when I was young, and with it we'd drink a large jug of sugary lime juice. We'd sit around eating and drinking while the elders were chatting. Here's an updated recipe using maple syrup as a flavouring. I think it's top of the pops!

Serves 2–4

25g (1oz) unsalted butter

2 tbsp maple syrup

½ tbsp vegetable oil

50g (1¾oz) popping corn

1. Melt the butter in a small saucepan over a medium heat, then stir in the maple syrup.

2. Heat the vegetable oil in a large saucepan with a lid set over a medium heat for 30 seconds, then add the corn and cover. After a few minutes you will hear popping. After about a minute, shake the pan and repeat every 30 seconds or so until the popping dies down. Turn off the heat and leave for 15 seconds more, to make sure the popping has stopped.

3. Pour the maple syrup and butter mixture over the corn, stirring it all together to combine, and serve immediately.

200

APPLE CRISPS

These are so full of flavour – they really shout 'it's ME!' I like them as a snack, and you can also have them on top of yogurt or porridge for breakfast.

Serves 2–4

25g (1oz) light muscovado sugar

25g (1oz) caster sugar

50ml (2fl oz) water

juice of 1 lime

¼ tsp ground cinnamon

3 eating apples (red ones look the best)

1. Preheat the oven to 120°C/fan 100°C/gas mark ½. Line 2 large baking sheets with nonstick baking paper.

2. Heat the sugars, water and lime juice in a small saucepan set over a low heat. Bring to the boil and simmer, stirring occasionally, until the sugars have dissolved. Increase the heat and boil for 4 minutes, or until the mixture is syrupy. Stir in the cinnamon.

3. Halve, core and thinly slice the apples. Dip the apple slices into the syrup and lay them on the baking sheets. Bake for 4 hours. These keep well in an airtight container.

COCONUT DROPS

Coconut drops are a typical Jamaican sweet – a wonderful cluster of coconut pieces stuck together with sugar.

Makes 10

140g (5oz) fresh coconut flesh

250ml (9fl oz) water

1 ½ tbsp peeled and coarsely grated fresh root ginger

200g (7oz) light muscovado sugar

pinch of salt

1. Line a baking sheet with nonstick baking paper. Finely dice the coconut and put it in a large, heavy-based saucepan set over a medium heat (the mixture rises up as it cooks so the pan must be big enough to accommodate this). Add the remaining ingredients and bring to the boil. Boil, stirring occasionally (and taking care not to burn your hand on the hot sugar), for around 15 minutes, or until the mixture is thick and sticky but not caramelized.

2. Drop 10 tablespoons of the mixture onto the lined baking sheet and leave to set.

DRINKS

CRISIS (Version)
(R. Marley)
PRODUCED BY BOB MARLEY
& THE WAILERS
Taken from the forthcoming album
"Kaya" – ILPS 9517

Rondor Music
Ltd

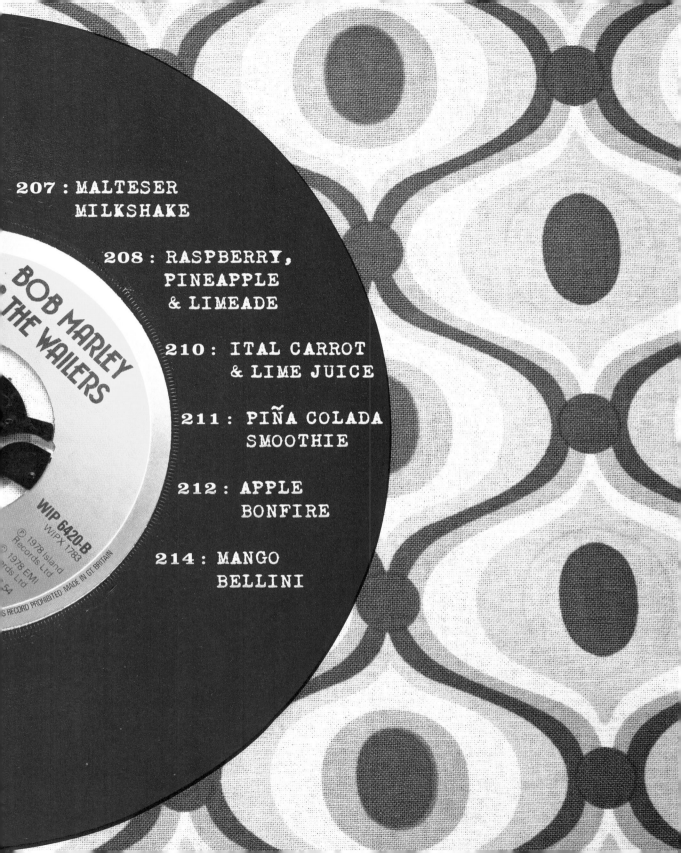

207 : MALTESER
MILKSHAKE

208 : RASPBERRY,
PINEAPPLE
& LIMEADE

210 : ITAL CARROT
& LIME JUICE

211 : PIÑA COLADA
SMOOTHIE

212 : APPLE
BONFIRE

214 : MANGO
BELLINI

This brings out the kid in me.
Put some brandy or rum in there, too,
if you want to make it more sophisticated.

MALTESER MILKSHAKE

Serves 2

- 300ml (½ pint) milk
- 1 tsp cocoa powder
- 1 tsp malted-milk drinking powder, such as Ovaltine
- 85g (3oz) Maltesers
- ½ tsp vanilla extract
- 6 ice cubes

1. Put all of the ingredients into a liquidizer, reserving 8 Maltesers for decoration. Whizz until well blended, then pour into chilled glasses.

2. Lightly crush the reserved Maltesers, scatter over the milkshakes and serve with coloured straws.

Wow, Lordahmercy, what a taste – sweet, tart and zingy. You don't have to use soda water – you can use bottled sparkling water, or even plain tap water if you don't mind not having fizz. You can also use mango or apple juice instead of pineapple juice.

RASPBERRY, PINEAPPLE & LIMEADE

Makes 1.4 litres (2½ pints)

450g (1lb) raspberries

55g (2oz) caster sugar, plus extra to taste (optional)

juice of 10 limes

250ml (9fl oz) pineapple juice

1 litre (1¾ pint) soda water, chilled

ice cubes, to serve

pineapple leaves, to decorate (optional)

1. Put the raspberries and 4 tbsp of the sugar in a bowl. Stir gently, cover, and set aside for 1 hour.

2. Transfer the raspberries to a food processor, add the remaining sugar, and whizz to a purée. Push the mixture through a nylon sieve into a jug, then mix in the lime and pineapple juices, and soda water, and stir in the ice. Add more sugar, to taste, if you want.

3. Serve in chilled glasses, decorated with pineapple leaves, if you like.

ITAL CARROT & LIME JUICE

Carrots are what's called 'ital', or 'vital'. Just seeing the bright colour of carrot juice makes me feel cheerful! Natural, delicious and good for you in every way, this drink offers a great way to get your 'ital' kick, morning, noon or night.

Serves 6

40g (1½oz) fresh root ginger, peeled and roughly chopped

150ml (¼ pint) freshly squeezed orange juice (about 4 oranges)

juice of 1 lime

2 tbsp soft light brown sugar

750ml (1⅓ pint) carrot juice

6 lime slices, to serve

1. Put all of the ingredients except the carrot juice and lime slices into a liquidizer and whizz to combine. Strain the mixture into a jug to remove any large pieces of ginger, pressing down on the pulp to extract as much flavour from the ginger as possible.

2. Pour the carrot juice into the jug and stir well to combine. Cover and chill in the refrigerator for at least 30 minutes.

3. To serve, pour into glasses and decorate with slices of lime. Drink and feel the get-up-and-go run through your veins.

PIÑA COLADA SMOOTHIE

Fresh and zingy, this is basically piña colada without the booze — so you can drink it at any time. It's best to serve it immediately as the juice and coconut cream can separate if left to stand.

Serves 4

400g (14oz) fresh pineapple
200g (7oz) coconut cream
200ml (⅓ pint) pineapple juice
50g (1¾ pint) Greek yogurt
juice of ½ lime
4 tbsp demerara sugar,
    or to taste
crushed ice, to serve (optional)

1. Put all of the ingredients into a liquidizer and whizz. That's it! All you need to do is taste to see if the smoothie has enough sugar for your liking (I'd be surprised if it didn't!).

2. Pour into glasses (preferably over crushed ice) and serve immediately.

APPLE BONFIRE

Serves as many as you like

- 1 part dark rum
- 2 parts apple brandy
- 4 parts apple juice (use clear apple juice rather than cloudy)
- dash of crème de cassis
- 2.5cm (1in) piece of cinnamon
- cinnamon sticks, to serve (optional)

The best winter warmer I can think of – apart, perhaps, from a big mug of hot chocolate with rum! Don't allow the mixture to boil otherwise you'll burn off all the alcohol.

1. Heat the liquids and 2.5cm (1in) piece of cinnamon together in a saucepan set over a medium heat. Bring almost to the boil, then reduce the heat and simmer for 5 minutes.
2. Share between heatproof mugs and serve with cinnamon sticks as stirrers, if you like.

MANGO BELLINI

There are no hard-and-fast rules for the mango purée in this – it really does depend on the flavour of your mangos. There's such a variety of mango tastes, so try different ones as they come into season. Sometimes I use the juice of just 1 lime, and sometimes I add a little sugar as well. Follow your taste.

Serves 6

1 large, ripe mango
juice of 2 limes, or to taste
caster sugar, to taste
75cl bottle Prosecco

1. Place 6 Champagne flutes in the freezer to chill. Peel and stone the mango and put the flesh into a liquidizer. Add the lime juice and purée until smooth. (You will have to keep taking the lid off and pushing the fruit down the sides of the liquidizer with a rubber spatula to make sure it all gets perfectly blended.)

2. Strain the mango purée through a sieve into a bowl. Add more lime juice or even a little sugar to taste. Chill in the coldest part of the refrigerator until really cold.

3. Pour the mango purée into a large jug. Add the Prosecco and gently whisk to blend. Pour the mixture into the chilled flutes and serve immediately.

Perfect for passionate encounters

Ride Natty Ride

ONE LOVE

Index

Levi's favourite fridge bar 57
pineapple & rum frangipane
    tart 76
pineapple & rum granita 181
roast apple, rum & maple fool 101
rum & raisin fudge 196
rum & toffee-apple ice cream 168
rum babas 122
tropical dried fruit salad 135
tropical fruit cake 20
vanilla rice pudding with cherry &
    rum syrup 91
walk the plank ice cream 172

salted caramel cheesecake 79
scented fruit salad 136
semolina
    coconut biscuits 47
shortbread
    billionaire's shortbread 43
    coconut biscuits 47
shortcake
    strawberry & mango shortcake 45
sorbets
    passion fruit & orange sorbet 176
    pineapple & rosewater sorbet 179
soufflé, passion fruit & orange 116
spiced chocolate-dipped fruits 190
spiced plum tart 64
stem ginger ice cream with hot
    chocolate topping 171
strawberries
    berry passion 133
    eatin' mess 84
    elderflower jelly trifle 150
    exotic fruit tart 69
    fruit cocktail, Caribbean style 130
    orange & Curaçao scented
        strawberries 134
    strawberry & banana coconut
        crumble 110
    strawberry & honey-pineapple
        fruit lollies 185
    strawberry & mango shortcake 45
sugar
    flamed sugar citrus fruits 157
    passionate muscovado
        bananas 161

sultanas
    chocolate & ginger tiffin 54
    Texan dollies 48
sundaes
    banana chocolate rum sundae 94
    ginger toffee apple sundae 96

tamarind
    honey & tamarind cake with lime
        icing 18
    tamarind balls 194
tarts
    boozy prune & almond tart 70
    Caribbean Bakewell tart 72
    exotic fruit tart 69
    ginger & lime treacle tart 71
    mango tarte tatin 63
    pineapple & rum frangipane
        tart 76
    spiced plum tart 64
tea
    tropical dried fruit salad 135
Texan dollies 48
thumbprint cookies 44
thyme
    figs with thyme-infused honey &
        Greek yogurt 158
tiramisu, Jamaican 87
toffee
    ginger toffee apple sundae 96
    rum & toffee-apple ice
        cream 168
trifles
    elderflower jelly trifle 150
    ginger & pear trifle 88–9
tropical butterfly cakes 30
tropical dried fruit salad 135
tropical florentines 40
tropical fruit cake 20

vanilla
    billionaire's shortbread 43
    fire-roasted peaches 162
    Levi's love buns 32
    Levi's pecan pie 74–5
    orange & Curaçao scented
        strawberries 134

pineapple & chilli upside-down
    cake 108
thumbprint cookies 44
vanilla rice pudding with cherry &
    rum syrup 91
white chocolate & vanilla cake
    with dark chocolate swirls 24

walk the plank ice cream 172
walnuts
    Texan dollies 48
white chocolate & raspberry
    sponge 27
white chocolate & vanilla cake with
    dark chocolate swirls 24

yogurt
    almond cake with lime &
        cardamom syrup 19
    eatin' mess 84
    figs with thyme-infused honey &
        Greek yogurt 158
    piña colada smoothie 211

Acknowledgements

I'd like to thank my children
Jo-anne, Danai, Zaion, Sharlene,
Bernice, Natalie and Tyran.
Thanks also to Hattie Ellis,
Diana Henry, Pene Parker,
Chris Terry, photographic
assistant Danny, Sara Lewis,
all the team at Mitchell
Beazley, Jake Brocklehurst,
John Eastaff, Rodney Levine-
Boateng, Natasha Eggough,
Borra Garson and Emma Hughes.

One love, Levi Roots

WELCOME!

Contents

The Gruff Guide to Monstro City

Roary Scrawl here, welcoming you to a super-smashing, rotten egg-cracking new year in Monstro City. As the editor of *The Daily Growl*, I'm always hearing about the latest fangtastic things our city has to offer. So get off your comfy Rocking Chair and prepare yourself for a year of monsterlicious madness, by reading my one and only Gruff Guide to Monstro City. Follow my dos and do-nuts, and you'll be raking in the Rox, and climbing the ranks of the Super Moshis in no time at all . . .

Monstro City:
Gruff Guide Dos and Do-nuts

DO keep your eyes peeled

There are new buildings being constructed, new monsters arriving, and new things happening every day in Monstro City. Blink and you might miss them! So always keep your eyes at hand and leave no Rox unturned until you find an adventure to go on.

DO NOT peel your eyes like you would a Zoot Fruit

It's not good, it's not clever, it's incredibly difficult to do and also pretty painful.

DO eat good food

Before a big day of exploring the city (so that's every day really), eat lots of powerful food fuel. A big luscious lump of Green, washed down with a hearty Cup O Gruel, will help keep you nourished for hours of arduous adventure. Head to the Gross-ery store and stock up. It's guaranteed to stop all those rumbling 'I'm monSTARving' tummy grumbles.

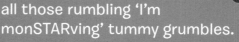

DO NOT have a messy home

A monster's home is their palace, so keep your room fit for the adventurer you are. Every keen explorer should bring back all their finds from their travels and show

them off to anyone who is interested! Fill your room with Tribal Masks, Dino Bones and everything else you can find of interest. It'll keep you constantly in the mood for adventure!

DO make friends

Adventures are always more fun with friends to scare (sorry, I meant share) them with. Make lots of new friends and tell them about your adventures in Monstro City. The other added bonus to having your own crew, is that the more friends you have, the better chance you'll have of becoming monSTAR of the week. And every good adventurer should be in the headlines at ALL times.

DO become a Super Moshi

Everyone's Super Moshi-dupering it, but they still need your help. If you are given the amazing opportunity to become one of the task force, then you go, monster, go!

DO NOT
sit at home all day twiddling your toes

Some days it may seem like a crazy monster-eat-monster world out there, but if you don't go and see what's around, you'll never know what you're missing. Try to get outside at least once every day, take a deep breath and smell the potent perfume of Monstro City's air. I promise you'll feel so much better for it.

DO get the right gear

To be a true eggsplorer, you must buy yourself a Scrambled Egg(splorer) Backpack to keep all your stuff in. Also, do remember that if you want to go on a top secret mission, you must never leave your house without your very own Black Shades and Fake Tash. You must look completely inconspicuous at ALL times.

So, now you should be totally ready for a year of adventure in Monstro City. Turn the page and begin!

New Year, New You

Welcome, Tyra Fangs here. It's the beginning of the year in Monstro City and what better time to think of some new year's resolutions for your Moshi Monster? Fill in my 'New Year, New Moshi Me' profile below, then look back at it at the end of the year and see if you stuck to your resolutions. Can you see into the future like my friend Agony Ant?

New Year, New Moshi Me

Moshi Name: _Rubyroxeyrock_

I would like to have _all_ Moshlings by the end of the year.

This year, my favourite Moshi Fun Park games will be: _Pet groomer_

This year, I will continue to be/become a Super Moshi, solving mysterious mysteries and helping out Monstro City. (Please circle as appropriate)

YES   NO

This year, I will be (mostly) wearing: _____

This year, my monster fave colour will be: _lime green + aqua blue_

This year, I will be shopping mainly at: _grossery store + YUCKEA_

This year, my top monster bands to dance to will be: (Circle them below)

Lady Goo Goo	The Goo Fighters	Banana Montana	Taylor Miffed
The Groanas Brothers	49 Pence	Brocolli Spears	
Pussycat Poppets	The Fizzbangs	Hairosniff	

This year, my monster tunes to listen to will be: _____

This year, my MonSTAR room rating will be: (Circle the number of stars you think your room rating will be this year.)

★★★★★

Have a MonSTAR-licious year, Moshis!
TF your BFF XXXXX

8

NEW YEAR, NEW YOU, NEW HOUSE

The perfect new accessory for a 'new year's new you' totally has to be a new house to chill in, dine in, party in and show off! So head on down to Ooh La Lane and pop into Monstro City's top estate agents, New Houses. There you will find everything from scarily cool city cribs to cute country bumpkin builds. Whatever you choose, make sure it's right for the new you . . .

Cake House Style
You'll be deliciously delighted with this home **sweeeeet home,** if your new year is about living life to the full – full-up that is! This **home-baked treat** really is the icing on the cake. If you keep extending up, it'll be the cherry on the top too!

Tree House Style
If this year your Moshi feels like swinging from one adventure to the next, the Tree House may be just what the jungle ordered. Perfect as a Super Moshi **super-secret hideout,** and complete with its very own **rope swing and ladder,** your Moshi will be climbing to the treetops in no time. (Only available from certain 'branches' of New Houses.)

Princess Castle Style
This year is **all about spoiling you,** your lovely little Moshlings and all your BFFs totally and utterly rotten, so buy the Princess Castle! Imagine running around the halls playing hide-and-seek with your pretty little friends, and washing your pinky pinkness in the wondrous waterfall – it's **picture perfect** and you know it, Princess!

Haunted House Style
Is your Moshi's resolution to scare everyone totally and utterly silly? If so, these **spooky surroundings** are dark night right for you. With creepy creaky doors and permanent night-time sky, these **deviant dwellings** will see to it that all your guests will be made frightfully uncomfortable. Mwah, ha, ha, Moshis!

Skyscraper Style
If your Moshi's life this year is on the up, keep on going upwards in this **sleek and slinky** Monstro-city apartment. Get those foundations right and you can **build, build, build** up to the top. (Really just to annoy your neighbours and ruin their views of the gloriously grey city streets below.)

Mountain House Style
Looking for a nice **relaxing retreat** this year? Well, look no further than the top of a mountain (you may need to buy some binoculars to help you out). Here you'll find a perfect room with a view, a cow and even your **very own hayloft** that you can use for . . . well, something exciting!

Moshi Style
If your Moshi's new year's resolutions are about spending your well-earned Rox on presents for others and helping out, perhaps a more **moderate and modest** abode is for you? With its **rustic charm** and back-to-basics building, you'll feel right at home with Moshi Style. Of course you will, it's your home!

Extend! Extend! Extend!

If you're in the mood for grand designs, add a second level to your home, or a third, or a fourth. You go, Moshi! After all, it's a new-year, new-you, new-house world!

Moe's Home Makeover

Are you bored of your bedroom, but daunted by DIY and scared silly of shopping? Fear no more, this year our very own Moe Yukky is here to help you get your room shipshape and sharp. Follow Moe's monstrous top ten makeover tips and you'll be cackling your way back to Yukea in no time!

1
Be modern
Keep up with the times by choosing between the curvy pink, brown or blue windows and doors. They're curvy (but of course) and very futuristic, so you'll never fall behind with your room chic again. That is until the future goes out of fashion, and I'll be sure to let you know when it does.

2
You too can have wondrous walls
And it's the bitter the better this season, so go for the Citrus Yellow Wallpaper for a tangtastic lemon look.

3
Store your junk
Tidy everything away and go green – grab a Green Cabinet and check out the top tips on going green on page seventeen!

4
Fabulous floors
Right now it's gotta be Yukea's Checker or Spotty floors for me – they're flawless.

5
Hot is cool
Buy the sizzling Fried Egg Rug and it'll be so smokin' hot in your room you could fry an egg. The key thing here is that you'll be hot whether you like it or not and, let's face it, who doesn't want to be hot?!

6
Improve your star rating
This one is pretty simple, just add more stars to your room yourself with one Star Rug, or two, or three. Ooh, aah, what a monSTAR you are!

7 Purple was the new black
And here at Yukea we are bringing it back with a Purple Chair where you can sit in purple comfort. Or try the Purple Table that turns everything you drink, well, er, purple! What we're saying is, 'Black, smack! Purple's back!'

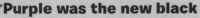

8 There's nothing like the real thing
Fakes never look good, so buy the Foot Table – as it's now made with genuine feet.

9 Finishing touches
Add a touch of sparkle to your life and your room with Yukea's beautiful chandelier. With its clanking chains holding glowing lanterns, you'll never be left in the dark about your room again!

10 Put your feet up
Tired from all that shopping and listening to my tips? Buy just one last thing for the day and make it a Monster Pouffe. Take my final words of advice and just relax after all that hard work buying stuff!

YUKEA

All You Need is Luvli

14th FEB

The Gift Island Gift Shop is the perfect place for sending cards, presents and letting people know how you feel. And the most perfect time of year for telling your furry friends you love them has to be Valentine's Day! Make and decorate your very own Luvli Moshi cards by copying the templates on the opposite page and choosing from the Luvli love messages below.

I ♥ you!

You're a super mon☆

Will you be my mon☆ friend?

You're my favourite mon☆ !!!

We are BMF!

♥ YOU ROX!

You send me Moshi mad!

SPONSORED BY GIFT ISLAND

You don't have to use these cards just for Valentine's Day, you can show someone how much you like or love them at any time of year, especially on their **burpdays!**

Drop Dead Gorgeous

Tyra Fangs, here again, and this time I'm here to tell you how to look and feel like the gorgeous new Moshi you are. This year, Monstro City's Katsuma Katzwalk was all about reflecting your mood and individuality, so today I want you to concentrate on getting your colours to reflect your monster's mood. After that, I'll show you how to top that all off with this season's hot new accessories.

In Da Mode for Fashion

The best way to find your individuality is by exploring your mood. Catwalk down to the Port, glide into Colorama and stand underneath the shower to see where the spraying takes you. Are you up for rosy-pink toes and luminous green eyes, or simply ready to blanket yourself in blackity, black, black? Try on lots of colours to see what you feel reflects your Moshi mood and use my colour chart below to help.

You can play with **MILLIONS of colour combos** for as long as you like! When you've found that purrrfect look, click on 'BUY' to pay for your paint and save your new colours. And don't worry if you feel like having your old self back again, just press 'WASH' and you'll be the same colour as before.

TYRA'S COLORAMA CHART

BLUE — spacey, dreamy, free, lazy

YELLOW + ORANGE — happy, lively, energetic, friendly, positive

GREEN — energetic, excited, jealous, natural

BLACK + GREY — chic, moody, mysterious, scary

RED — determined, strong, dangerous, rich

PURPLE — spooky, individual, different, luxurious

PINK — girly, cheery, sweet, sugary

Don't forget you can adjust the brightness of each colour, too!

14

Essential Accessories!

Now you have your colour sorted, some uber-necessary accessories will complete the perfect individual drop-dead gorgeous monster look.

1. SWEAT BAND
– Sweat but don't wanna get wet, Poppet? This is for you.

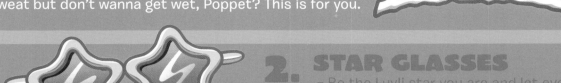

2. STAR GLASSES
– Be the Luvli star you are and let everyone know, with these funky star glasses.

3. THE WIZARD OF SNOZ BEARD
– Beards are mandatory for all Snoz Wizards and Furis alike.

4. FINGERLESS GLOVES
– Get these snipped-off gloves on and rebel against the monster, Zommer.

5. CAT EARS
– For all Diavlo cats. Miaaaaow, purr, purr, purr, purr. Woof, woof. Wait, that's a dog. Well, you get the cat's eye-dear.

MARKETPLACE Monstro City

NOW OPEN!

Packed full of boutique shops to suit every monster's needs (and even stuff every monster doesn't really need at all, but is just a lot of fun!).

COME GRIME WITH ME

March is the time to celebrate Growly Grub Day. What better way to celebrate it than with tips for the perfect monster food combos and monster entertaining tips for any occasion?

T is for Two

It's always lovely to share some tea with a friend (as long as you have enough food to eat yourself as well!). Take a look at our top Moshi Ts below. (Note: These should all be served with tea from Mr. Tea – coffee-drinking at T-Time is for fools!) These menus are sooooo filling that you will be just about happy enough to share them.

MENU

Bangers and Mash:
This explosive dinner is bound to go down with a bang at your dining table! Just hopefully not with a bang in your tummies, too!

Fly Trap Salad:
Perfect for feeding guests you want to stay trapped with you for quite some time. One bite, and it'll bite them back!

Jelly Baked Beans mixed with Mutant Sprout:
The perfect combo, for those who like the weather – windy days in particular.

Super Moshi Super Food Supper

It's all about the power. Should you have the Super Moshis over for a Super Supper, then load up the Green stuff and build up their energy, so they are ready to go out and fright another day.

The key ingredients for a Super Moshi Supper are:

A big chunk of Green and some Mutant Sprouts for goodness.

A Quenut Butter Sandwich for energy.

Starlight Cookies for superstar power!

Party Grub

Sickly, snazzy, snacky food for entertaining at parties:

Toad Soda – cheap and simple party fizz, bang, wallop!

Slug Slurp Slushies – pretty packaging with pink straws and slithering slugs, what more could any party gal ask for?

Swirlberry Muffins – your friends are sure to have a swirl time with these on the table!

SPONSORED BY THE GROSS-ERY STORE

17th MARCH

KEEPING GREEEEEEN

In honour of St Patrick's Day, why not try buying, wearing, eating and decorating entirely in green? See below for all the gorgeously green things you might be able to get your grubby green paws on.

GRUBBY GREEN CUISINE:

Green (big lump of green)

Roast Beast (Green)

Slime Rickey

Eat the plant part of Eggplant only

Only drink Croak-a-cola's Toad Soda all day

GREEN GENES:

Green Feather Boa – how lush!

Green Shades – everything will be a shade greener

Wear a green Weremon Shirt

Green toe-ripped flippers (made from hardened green)

THE GREEN, GREEN GRASS OF HOME:

Grab a Broccoli Spears poster for your wall

Green Swirl Wallpaper from Horrods

Plant some Magic Green Beans in your Moshling garden

Grassy or Leaves Window from the DIY Store

GREEN FIENDS:

Only hang out with green friends or buy yourself a Cuddly Ecto

How green are you? Head into Monstro City and see how many green things you can buy. Write the number here:

Interview with a Monster

Roary Scrawl's Interview Tips

As the main editor of *The Daily Growl*, I have interviewed many a monster in my time and have pretty much talked my way through everything! Here are my top tips to awesome monster interviews.

Flip the book over to read Roary's scrawl!

★ Research your subject. It would be most embarrassing if you knew nothing about who you were interviewing before they arrived. For example, I can't see Simon Growl being too impressed if you were to ask him what his job was, can you?

★ Prepare your questions beforehand. That way, you will get exactly what you want out of the interview and not a bin full of rubbish facts like what they ate for breakfast that day.

★ Keep your eyes on the prize! It helps that I have loads of eyes to do so, but take it from me, you'll remember a lot more if you actually look closely at who you are interviewing. If you don't, it just seems rude and they might simply run away without you noticing, and then you'd be in trouble.

★ Use simple questions and keep to the point. Some monsters, like good old Cap'n Buck, have very little time to stand around nattering all day. They have adventures to go on and treasure to find, me hearties!

★ Keep your questions open. Don't ask any questions that will mean you get a simple yes or no answer.

★ Be polite and always thank whoever you are interviewing at the end, even if they have been completely and utterly useless! Once, I interviewed Monstro City's first yodelling fish, and all she did was sing 'She sells sea shells,' throughout the whole interview. Nevertheless, I thanked her for her time. You never know when a yodelling fish may come in handy for something. Happy interviewing, my roving reporters!

ROARY SCRAWL'S QUESTION GRIME WITH CAP'N BUCK

 RS: Cap'n Buck is back and HERE! Buck took the time to catch up with me and tell all about his newest adventures and booty from Tiki Tropic.

Hello, Cap'n Buck! How was Tiki Tropic?

 CB: It be very adventurous indeed! There be a big storm.

 RS: Oh no, are you okay?

 CB: Of course! I am an expert at manning th' ship in th' storms and it was worth it for all th' treasures I did find ye.

 RS: Phew, that's a relief. Well now, let's get down to beeswax . . . Tell us what you brought back from Tiki Tropic!

 CB: I won't tell ye everythin', but I will say that I brought one of me favourite treasures so far. Here's a clue: They be very dark, but used in light and not very helpful at night.

 RS: Ok! I'm SO heading to the port to see what you have right now! Thanks Cap'n Buck! See you again soon!

Head to The Port to see Cap'n Buck's latest bootiful booty finds!

Can you guess what Cap'n Buck's treasure from Tiki Tropic was? Go to page 60 to find out if you were right.

MIGHTY MOSHI MONTH

There are so many things worth celebrating in April. Read our top tips to celebrating every Monstro City April occasion in style!

Happy Pranksgiving!

Start April off jumping for joy, with the hilarious arrival of Pranksgiving. You'd better be prepared for some **side-splitting silliness!** Pranksgiving is the one and only time of the year when every monster is allowed to play pranks on all their pals. In fact, it's the only day when you simply must play pranks, otherwise you'll be seen as a Pranksgiving party pooper and that would s'not be cool! So join in the jovial times, by telling everyone your **jolliest jokes** ever, leaving fantastically funny messages on your friends' notice boards, sending slightly scary but extremely amusing gifts to your mates and laugh, laugh, laugh, like you've never laughed before. **Mwah, ha, ha, ha!**

Write down your funniest Pranksgiving joke here, then send it in to *The Daily Growl* next year for all monsters to read and enjoy:

Write down the funniest prank played on you on past Pranksgivings here:

Ha Ha Ha Ha!

Jelly Bean Day

It's THE day for **jellybeans!** To **celebrate this jelliness** of a day, you must eat everything you can find with jellybeans in it, and surround yourself with all that is jelly and all that be bean.

Start the day off nicely with a lovely big bubbly bowl of **Jelly Baked Beans** from the Gross-ery Store. Then add a **Yellow Jelly Floor** to your room and plaster your walls with some limited edition **Jelly Bean Wallpaper**. Stock up on lots of **Crab and Jelly**

Sandwiches then **invite your friends over** to hang out on your **Heart-shaped Bean Bag** and eat them all. Make sure that everyone wears their Blue Cat Beanie Hats and that they admire your collection of **Beanie Blobs**. Enjoy chatting about where you have all 'bean' recently and what you've 'bean' up to. Jelly Bean Day celebrations are bound to have everyone 'beaning' for joy. So jump around like a jumping jellybean and enjoy. Your day will be **simply jellyishious!**

Roy G Biv Day

Roy G Biv is a professional Rainbow Rider, an expert Sky Surfer and a Colossal Cloud Cruiser! He is **totally cool and colourful**, and only graces Monstro City with his presence once a year on Roy G Biv Day. He comes to our shores to make sure there are rainbows over Monstro City all year round, even without any rain!

Celebrate Roy G Biv Day, by surrounding yourself in colour and rainbow-dellic radness! Wear your brightest clothes, buy a Rainbow Stand to get all the colours of the rainbow all of the time, find the end of the rainbow by sitting on a Rainbow Chair (the end is where you are sitting, of course), buy yourself a Rainbow Painting or paint yourself all kinds of colours. Finally, make everything **technicolour funtastic** by sporting a pair of Rainbow Shades!

Top Tip: Remember to watch out for Roy G Biv's FunkyFuchsiaFakie too!

Earth Day

Earth Day is a very special day for celebrating the birth of Earth. And what's a good name for Earth's birthday? Earth Day, of course! So, take some time out today to think about all the things you can do to help your planet. It could be to remind yourself to **recycle, recycle, recycle,** turn lights out and toys off when you are not using them, not drop any rubbish on the streets, give your old 'too small for you' clothes to someone else, or even plant lots of Luvli luscious things in your garden. Whatever you decide to do, remember that every little thing will help to **save the globe** and keep your planet clean and green for you and your friends, for MonSTAR-light years to come!

Make three thrifty new Earth Day resolutions to help the environment and write them down here:

Turn the page to learn more about what you can invent with your unwanted Moshi items . . .

21

ABSOLUTELY RUBBISH!

After celebrating Earth Day, your mind is probably bursting with lots of rubbish! Rubbish that you want to recycle, that is. What should you do with it? Get some inspiration from Monstro City's list of alternative and creative ways of using old or unwanted monster junk! Some crazy inventions may be afoot - literally!

Myrtle's Marvellous Swirlberry Muffin Stand

World-renowned for her treasure-hunting ability, Myrtle the Diving Turtle is very resourceful. Her most inventive invention to date has to be her suave, sophisticated and super-swell Swirlberry Muffin Stand. It's made of piles of very used broken plates found at the bottom of the sea, put together in a giant tower and stuck together with . . .

. . . Giuseppe Gelato's Glue

Ever worried about what happens to all of that leftover ice scream at the end of the day? Well, do not fear - Giuseppe's ingenious business brain is here! Giuseppe is now using all his extra sticky-wicky ice scream, as sticky-wicky glue. So far, G G Glue has only been used on Myrtle's Marvellous Swirlberry Muffin Stand, but it could be used for anything and everything that needs to be stuck together, sticky-wicky-like - just remember to read the Manufacturer's Note.

Manufacturer's Note: This glue will melt in approximately thirty seconds if not kept in arctic conditions at ALL times.

Dizzee Bolt's Helicopter Hard Hat

Maintaining the nuts and bolts of the EN-GEN system is tough work for Dizzee, but she and her great engine-ious mind have found time to fit in some inventing.

Monsters everywhere will love their very own Helicopter Hard Hat. Fitted with helicopter blades for flying, one million Monstrowatts of energy and a hat for your head - it's absolutely every monster's dream machine!

Please read the safety instructions carefully before use . . .

Safety Instructions: Helicopter Hard Hats are not suitable for anyone under (or over) the age of 100. Possible side effects of wearing them include a permanent fear of flying and fear of wearing hats.

My Recycled Monstrous Invention

Have a look at all the junk you have in your monster's inventory and invent something new to do with it here:

Super Glooper Day

Everyone LOVES Super Glooper Day! And why wouldn't they? It's the day when we all eat Gloop, play games with Gloop, have Gloop fights and sing Gloop songs! What's not to Gloop? So sing along with this Super Gloop song, and show your dedication to the gloopity-gloop cause!

Gloop, Gloop, Gloopity-Gloop!
Gloop, Gloop, Gloopity-Gloop!

Step in it, swing it,
And slurp it through straws.
Serve it at parties,
And stash it in drawers.

Gloop, Gloop, Gloopity-Gloop!
Gloop, Gloop, Gloopity-Gloop!

Wriggle it, swiggle it,
Shovel it and scoop.
Gobble it, wobble it,
Make it into soup.

Gloop, Gloop, Gloopity-Gloop!
Gloop, Gloop, Gloopity-Gloop!

Throw it and blow on it,
Wear it on your head.
Stick it on the ceiling,
Tuck it into bed!

Gloop, Gloop, Gloopity-Gloop!
Gloop, Gloop, Gloopity-Gloop!

Chop it and flop it,
Stick it to your tongue.
Everyone can gloop it,
Even Super Glooper mums!

Gloop, Gloop, Gloopity-Gloop!
Gloop, Gloop, Gloopity-Gloop!

NOTE: Preferably to be sung whilst standing on one leg, and hopping around in a circle with Gloop Soup in one hand or foot. Must be repeated at least ten times for Super Glooper effect.

WHEN ON MAIN . . .

There are lots of little hidden things to spot in Monstro City. With all his eyes, Roary Scrawl can keep an eye on everything – literally. Check out *The Daily Growl* Guide to what's happenin' on da street and meet Monstro City's resident monsters.

The Daily Growl

All the ooze that's fit to print!

When on Main Street

⭐ Pick out the picnic monsters to play Moshling Boshling!

⭐ **Near the Flutterby Field is a boingy little monster. Can you find him?**

⭐ Startle the sleeping sandwich guy, Bjorn Squish. He has an **appetite for construction** and is always on his lunch break.

When on Ooh La Lane

⭐ Look for a drain that won't drain your energy, but will get you in the mood for dance **moves and groove** The musical notes will help you find the tune.

⭐ **Make the street lamps swing in th streets.**

⭐ Find a cutie cat, named Purr Fection, and see if you can wake he up from her slumber.

⭐ **Make the fountain come alive. Can you spot who flies out? Look carefully, it all happens in a splas**

⭐ **Make a wish** at the well, or just click on it and see what sinister happenings happen. Could it be Dr. Strangeglove, and is something strange going on with his glove? Stay close at hand, or glove, to see what's going on.

⭐ **Take some time to find a monster behind a clock face. Will he tell yo the time?**

When on Sludge Street

⭐ Go see Max Volume and his mega-amped boom box to see if you can get him to bust some moves.

⭐ Head to the water, where something fishy is going on. Or is it simply a boot? Go fishing with Billy Bob Baitman and see.

⭐ Can you spot Tiddles, the local legendary sea monster, and get him to yodel for you?

⭐ See the pumping shed? It might just be another way for you to hit the dance floor!

⭐ Need to get back to nature? Find Chomper and Stomper, the grass mowing moo-errs and hang out with them as they roam free. Mooo-err!

When at The Port

⭐ Click on poor little old Roland Jones, and his bottle of Tangy Tonic. Watch him make rather rude noises, as he tries to grow bigger . . .

⭐ Watch Lenny Lard in his rubber ring disappear under the water when you touch him. He may not be able to swim, but he sure can project himself out of the water faster than a rocket! Watch out!

⭐ Touch the lighthouse eye and watch her closely . . . Oh dear, looks like you blinked and missed it!

⭐ Give purple-licious Octo a bit of a nudge and i-spray what happens.

⭐ Find a little monster on the bridge and he'll give you a giggle and a wave.

When on Gift Island

⭐ Oh dear, that poor postman, Clutch, is carrying such a heavy load of presents. Click on him to see if you can help him out!

⭐ Try to find a little fella or two to cheer up on the rocks. Elwood and Bert may have something they want to show you, but they're a little shy.

How does your Moshling Garden Grow...?

...WITH SILLY PEPPERS ALL IN A ROW!

Are your Hot Silly Peppers looking a little cold and sensible? Has the fire from your Dragon Fruit gone out? Or are you just simply longing for green fingers to match your green clothes? Read these tips from Buster Bumblechops and Cluekoo, and you'll have your very own beautiful Moshling garden in 'grow' time at all!

Greetings, fellow Moshling hunters! Buster Bumblechops, Moshling expert extraordinaire at your service. Today I'm going to talk to you about creating the perfect Moshling-attracting garden.

Buster's Basics

So we all know we have a garden, right? Well then, that's rather a good start. Head to your garden and take a look at it and ask yourself these questions: Is it pretty? Would I like to live here? If the answer is no, then read on and learn how to make your garden the most attractive it can be, so you can have lots of lovely little Moshlings all to yourself!

Cluekoo's Clues

Buy some seeds on Main Street to plant in your garden or go to Super Seeds at The Port if you are a member.

Head to your garden from the sign at the cart or by going to the map and clicking on Moshling Garden.

MOSHLING SEEDS

Once all three flowers have grown, you'll see if you've attracted a Moshling.

Flowers take time to bloom, but remember that a happy monster's flowers grow the fastest. So keep your monster happy!

Plant a seed in each of the three plots of your garden and watch them grow.

Keep trying - there are Moshlings in the wild who like all sorts of flowers.

If you don't get a Moshling, don't worry. I'll give you a hint on how to find one.

Cluekoo's Crazy Combos

Try out some of these crazy combos to see what cool Moshlings you catch.

TIP - keep your eyes on the prize and read the sign at the Moshling Cart. If you are in desperate need of help and you don't have me to ask, click on the scarecrow.

BREAKING NEWS!

Do you dream of joining Roary on the newsdesk?
Fancy yourself as *The Daily Growl*'s hot new roving reporter?
Or maybe the sports pages are more your thing?

Now's your chance to create your own pages for Monstro City's favourite newspaper.
Hunt down the headlines, snoop out a story and draw in the pictures to go with it!
Then, have a go at the sports pages and invent your own level of Moshling Boshling!

All the ooze that's fit to print!

The Daily Growl

If you've never checked out Moshling Boshling, find the picnickers on Main Street and they will show you the way!

Moshling Boshling

Moshling Boshling is the sporting craze that's sweeping Monstro City! If you've cracked all the levels on Moshling Boshling already, then why not have a go at designing your own? Think carefully about where to position the cakes and the Glumps to give your players the maximum chance of hitting them all, without making it too easy!

WEEEEEEEEEEEEEE!
YIIIIIIIIIIKES!

What's that smell?

I believe that's Broccoli Spears by Kelvin Swine.

Tyra's perfume! I smell trouble. Tyra was here, but she must've been monster-napped!

They find the ferry in the middle of Potion Ocean, but no one seems to be onboard. There's just a faint whiff of . . .

e Super Moshis rch for more clues.

We've searched everywhere, left no stern unturned . . . the only thing we haven't done is . . .

. . . Open the presents!

Precisely.

I wonder what these tools are for?

We'd better keep a' hold of 'em, just in case.

C.L.O.N.C

Suddenly the anchor is hoisted up and the ferry begins to move with, ahem . . . no one at the helm!

?

Sizzlin' sailors! Who's sailing this ship?

Gift Island

RUMBLE, RUMBLE!

ithout a captain in sight, the Gift and Ferry sails onwards, and cks at the Moshi Fun Park.

he ferry must have been programmed. bt the programmer knew we'd be aboard! We have to find out why we are here.

WELCOME TO MOSHI FUN PARK GH

I wonder who GH is? Looks like Roary's scrawl, but he would be RS, wouldn't he?

Welcome! Tickets, please.

Flying fun parks! That's a shame.

But I bought tickets from Cap'n Buck. They have the letters 'O' and 'S' on them.

'O' and 'S' are the correct letters to get in. Please enter the Fun Park and have fun.

When the Super Moshis enter the park, they are handed a riddle from *The Daily Growl*.

What letter can you eat, drink and play golf with?

33

I wonder why we keep seeing strange letters? First 'G', then 'H' on the flag.

Then 'O' and 'S' on the tickets, and now...

Cuppa tea, anyone?

That's it! You can drink tea, eat tea, and hit a golf ball off of a tee. The answer to the riddle is the letter 'T'.

I wonder if all these letters mean anything? Maybe quiz master, Tamara Tesla, is trying to tell us something? G – H – O – S - T...

...GHOST! To the Ghost Train it is!

GHOST TRAIN

The team heads to the Ghost Train, for a monster of a ride ...

WOAH!
WOOOA
WOOOOOOOO

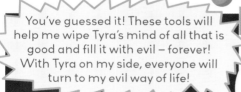

Fango Mandango, this is one crayzee ride!

CRASH!

BANG!

WALLOP-SPLAT!

I wasn't expecting you to bring the tool for my new machine. Mwa, ha, ha, ha Thank you for your help, Super Moshis

C.L.O.N.C

BRAIN SQUISH MACHINE

Maddening mash-ips! In trying to save Tyra, we've actually helped out Dr. Strangeglove!

You've guessed it! These tools will help me wipe Tyra's mind of all that is good and fill it with evil – forever! With Tyra on my side, everyone will turn to my evil way of life!

You won't get away with that. No one will believe you. Roary will tell everyone what you're doing in *The Daily Growl*.

I wouldn't be so sure about that, my little Super Moshi...

Just then, Roary Scrawl appeared.

I came to save Tyra, but the doctor has turned me into a slave. Thank goodness you followed the emergency trail I left.

Aha!

That's right, Moshis! I monster-napped Tyra to trap Roary and take over *The Daily Growl*. Soon, the whole of Monstro City will be mine! Mwah, ha, ha, ha!

Yodelling Furis! What are we going to do? Let's crack this case! Now, what weapons do we have?

Tentacle Torch

Silly Scissors

Supe Gloop Glue

Hmm, well we'll just have to make do. Now, split up!

Will Dr. Strangeglove turn everyon evil by morning and destroy Monstro City?

GLOOP!

SNIP!

KAPOW!

The Super Cart speeds off, leaving Dr. Strangeglove behind, and somewhat super-shocked.

Flying around the Fun Park at super speeds, the cart zooms over towards Main Street, landing . . .

ZOOOOMMMM!!!

just outside *The Daily Growl* offices.

The Daily Growl

The Daily Growl

Monstro City's Next Top Monster:
Dr. Strangeglove!

Tyra Wears Strange Gloves this Season!

Dr.Strangeglove top-tipped to win all of this year's Monster's Choice Awards!

Seeing the evil news pages just about to be printed, Roary shouts . . .

STOP!

Roary and Tyra set to work writing a new version of *The Daily Growl* in time for the morning.

The Super Moshis have saved the day once again!

The Daily Growl

Super Moshis save Tyra from Super Fashion Disaster!

New News in Nick of Time!
Beware Dr. Strangeglove still on lose.
Last seen underneath Moshi Fun Park.

Fun Park Ghost Train Ride:
Shut Until Further Notice

Lenny Lard Lost on Land

Fun Park Ghost Train:
Shut Until Further Notice

Further Notice

Do you think you have what it takes to become a Super Moshi? Read on for further instructions and good luck!

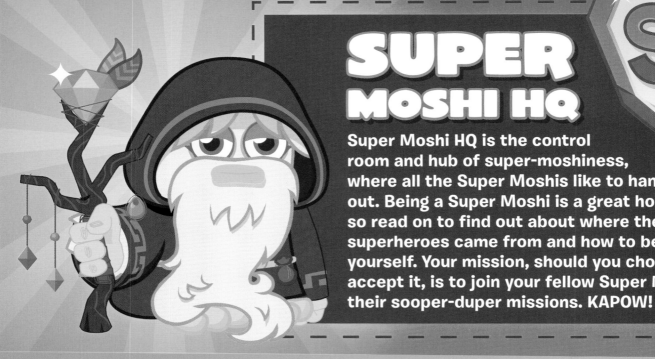

SUPER MOSHI HQ

Super Moshi HQ is the control room and hub of super-moshiness, where all the Super Moshis like to hang out. Being a Super Moshi is a great honour, so read on to find out about where the amazing superheroes came from and how to become one yourself. Your mission, should you choose to accept it, is to join your fellow Super Moshis on their sooper-duper missions. KAPOW!

One day, many moons ago, Moshi miners discovered an enormous underground cavern beneath Monstro City. Inside they found a huge glowing rock shaped like a wonky upside-down question mark that was shaking and juddering. Not knowing much at all about anything, the miners used their picks to shatter the rock. When it cracked open they found an entire tribe of **sleeping Super Moshis.**

Suddenly, the miners began discussing quantum physics, untangling their pretzels and helping each other make capes using empty Umba Thunk sacks. This was because the Super Moshis were giving off OoperDuper energy and wisdom waves, even when they were snoozing.

Before long, the Super Moshis **stirred from their slumber,** slammed their fists against their chests, pointed skywards and fell flat on their faces. Well, so would you if you'd been asleep that long! After a few push-ups and star jumps they got to work, dishing out nuggets of knowledge and teaching monsters **how to make friends** and get along. And that's the way it stayed for many years.

Then one day, having knocked a whole heap of sense into generations of monsters, the Super Moshis **suddenly disappeared.** No goodbyes, no leaving parties . . . nothing. Well, okay, they did stick a little note on the fridge saying 'Our work here is done' but it fell off. And that was that. Or so we thought.

Because (trumpet blast, please) Super Moshis are back, and they're ready to whup Monstro City into shape all over again.

WHAT ARE SUPER MOSHIS?

Super Moshis are all-seeing, all-knowing, cape-wearing champions of **Truth, Justice and the Moshi Way.** Failing that, think of them as smarty-pants who look really cool (even if some of 'em do wear their underwear over their clothes).

WHAT'S A SUPER MOSHI'S JOB?

- To be a SUPER role model
- Meet and greet new monster owners by friend-requesting them and sending them a **welcome message** on their Pinboard
- Help answer questions at the Moshi Forum
- Read *The Daily Growl* every day (hopefully you do that already!)
- Hype up Moshi contests in the Forum and on your Pinboard

NOTE: Don't worry, you won't have to wear underwear outside of your clothes. Unless you really want to, that is!

MOSHI MISSIONS

As a Super Moshi you will be sent on lots of exciting missions. When you are called up for a mission you should head to the Volcano, where the Gatekeeper will be waiting for you . . .

Moshi Missions

Mission 1: MISSING MOSHLING EGG

Buster Bumblechops has reported that a Moshling egg has been stolen from his Incubation Station. You must look for clues and find the missing egg.

In this mission, some of your egg-citing adventures will include:

- Searching Buster's room for **clues** to help find the thief
- Investigating the Wobbly Woods
- Enlisting the help of a goblin
- Finding a **secret hideout** and the skeleton key to open it, deep in the dark, spooky woods
- Making a magical potion to **shrink the egg**
- Returning the egg safely to Buster Bumblechops

Mission 2: VOYAGE UNDER POTION OCEAN

Strangeglove is stealing fish from the beach. Enlist the help of Cap'n Buck and discover Strangeglove's evil plan.

In this mission, some of your fishy adventures will include:

- Finding the rowing boat and paddling to Cap'n Buck's *Cloudy Cloth Clipper*
- Swabbing the poop deck and busting the barnacles
- Finding Buck's compass
- Sailing around islands to find a propeller
- Fixing the submarine
- Captaining the submarine to Strangeglove's underwater lair
- Destroying **Strangeglove's Glumping Machine**
- Rescuing Wurley the Techie Moshling

Mission 3: GET OFF OF MY CLOUD!

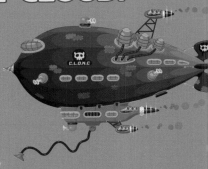

Strangeglove is sucking out Moshlings from the sky, using a giant hose from an airship! You must sneak on board the airship and destroy it.

In this mission, some of your flighty adventures will include:

- Using Wurley (the Moshling gained in Mission 2), you go **flying up into the clouds** in search of Strangeglove's airship
- Discovering that Cloud City is full of Fluffies and Sky Ponies that are being vacuumed up by Strangeglove
- **Chasing the airship** and avoiding the Glump Goo cannon fire
- Rescuing the Moshlings
- Destroying the airship!

Mission 4:
STICKY TOFFEE TURMOIL / CANDY CANE CALAMITY

You find out that several new food items that have appeared in the Gross-ery Store are making monsters sick. Can you solve the mystery?

In this mission, some of your sweet adventures will include:
- Heading to the Candy Cane Caves where players discover 'Sweet Tooth', a baddie who is **mining candy** and poisoning it
- Steering a runaway mine cart

Mission 5:
POP GOES THE GOOGOO!

Lady GooGoo has lost her voice and has a huge concert at Trembly Stadium. Strangeglove has been spotted at her gigs, papping away with a big camera. Is he responsible? Time to investigate!

In this mission some of your **rocking adventures** will include:
- Heading to Simon Growl's mansion
- Arranging musical notes in the right order
- Going to musical boot camp

Mission 6:
BACK TO SCHOOL

At the Super Moshi Academy, students are misbehaving and dropping out at an alarming rate. Go and investigate!

STOP PRESS!

At the time of going to print, mission 6 was still a mystery to the Super Moshis! Fill in the challenges you faced below:

Once you have completed these missions, be sure to keep a Super Moshi eye out for your next challenges!

39

Crafty Business

Follow the simple instructions to make your very own Glump!

YOU WILL NEED

- White and coloured cardboard
- Wool, the colour you would like your Glump to be
- Two circular objects to draw around, one bigger than the other, or a safe compass
- Safety scissors
- Sticky tape
- Glue

WHAT TO DO:

1.

First decide what type of Glump you want to make. The choice is all yours!

2.

Then, start making your Glump's body by drawing two doughnut shapes on a piece of card, as shown. Use your circular objects to make a big circle and then a little circle inside it, as shown.

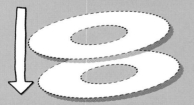

X 2

3.

Cut out the two large circles, then cut out the two smaller circles inside them and place the rings together.

4.

Cut your wool into lengths, then hold one end of the wool on the outside of the ring and feed the other through the middle holes of your doughnut shapes, wrapping the wool around the card.

5.

Repeat the above, until all the cardboard is covered. Each time you start a new length of wool, make sure the ends are on the outside of the circle.

6.

When you have just a smal hole left in the middle, spli the wool apart on the edge t find the cardboard and ask a grown up to cut the woo around the edges.

7.

Pass a length of wool between the pieces of cardboard, around the strands of wool and tie it together firmly.

8.

Take off the cardboard rings.

9.

Use the faces above to copy and draw onto your card. Then cut them out and attach them to your ball of wool to finish your Glump.

10.

Now repeat all the steps to make a friend for your Glump!

The Life of a Poshi Moshi

Want a life like Posh Mice? Feel like one is always a country-clubbing cut above the rest? Well, here's a chance to find out how to make one's monster's shopping, dressing and eating habits superbly extravagant. Go on, you simply must indulge . . .

Where to shop?

Where everything is just that little bit more **expensive and unaffordable!** So head to Horrods right now and shop til you drop. Remember to buy yourself lots of presents and show them off, so you look **spiffingly popular.**

Where NOT to shop

A posh Mosh would not be seen dead, alive or even walking in the vicinity of Bizarre Bazaar, Dodgy Dealz or the DIY store. Why? Because you would never do it yourself darling, not if there is someone else to do it for you!

How to decorate one's palace

As a **posh Mosh** you are most likely to own either a Princess Castle with all the princess trimmings, or an enormous 'eye saw it first' mansion of a skyscraper. Any other abodes would simply **not be good enough for you.** Once one has one's prize property, one must:

- Fill one's shiny shelves with divine statues
- Cover one's walls in bountiful black or rich purple Swirl Wallpaper from Horrods
- Add a Fishy Fountain centre piece to every room in one's mansion
- Show how rich one is by smothering one's walls in lashings of luxurious scary rarey art, such as the Scream Painting or Blimp Painting
- Add a Spider Chandelier to one's ballroom, kitchen, bedroom and even luxury on-sweet WC

What to wear

The key to a poshi Moshi's glamour status is to **keep up with fashion**, no matter what. If carrying your Moshlings around in an old trolley bag and wearing yellow shoes with a blue boa is in all the latest monster mags, then that is what you should be doing, too. Follow **Tyra's Terribly Posh Fashion Guide** here for some sickly rich suggestions:

- Always wear shades, even underground. They always look good
- Wear a Feathered Hat or Bowler Hat whilst in the country
- Always wear as much expensive jewellery as possible. Lots of Loop earrings should do the trick
- Platinum Pants of Power – because you're not silver, not gold, but platinum, baby!
- There is no such thing as too many Feather Boas, so buy all of them in every colour and let them hang off you with effortless style
- The Prince or Princess Headdress is an everyday essential for you
- Golden Tiara – everyone knows you're a princess, so just right royally roll with it!
- Stripy Bow Ties – some may wear these in jest, but they don't know any better
- Riding Hat – because you like everyone to know you have stables full of six-legged swildebeasts

What NOT to wear

- A Yellow Jump Suit – you do not want to appear like you actually have to do a day's work, when you do not
- Sweatband – you, break a sweat? No chance. You'll never need to wear one of these

Where to hang out

When not seen taking a stroll along Ooh La Lane or buying all that glitters from Horrods, one might **partake of some culture** at the Googenheim Art Gallery, and **browse for new estates** at New Houses, purely for investment purposes of course.

Posh Nosh (what to eat)

- A Sauce of Course – simply because you like saying 'of course'. It's rather posh
- Fango Mandango – because whatever it is, it sounds fancy, just like you!
- Grande Gateaux – because one is terribly grand, isn't one?
- Anything shiny and rich-looking

What not to be seen eating

- Bangers and Mash – just trash
- Spamburger - **no fast food** for you, it's all about slow food at the moment, and you have to be on trend even in what you eat
- Mutant Sprout – you are what you eat and that's all I'm saying. Don't do it!
- Slug Slurp Slushie – because **poshi Moshis don't slurp**, burp or anything of that revolting nature – in public at least – keep it in the Water Closet

TALK LIKE A PIRATE DAY

Shiver me timbers, it's Talk Like a Pirate Day! A day when we all, well, talk like a pirate! To give you a hook on this here special day, Cap'n Buck E. Barnacle has put together some useful words and phrases for ye.

PIRATE S'WORDS:

ahoy! – hello
aloft - upstairs
an' – and
avast - stop
aye – yes
aye, aye – of course, I will get to it
be – an, are or is
booty – riches that may have been stolen
canna – can't
cutlass - sword
didna – didn't
drink, the – Potion Ocean
fer – for
grub - food

hands - crew
hearties – friends
jabber - talk
Jolly Roger – pirate flag
lad – young monster pirate
lass – young lady monster
me - my
noggin - head
offe - off
ol' - old
ou' - out
pieces of eight (also known as booty. See left) – money/Rox
port - left
starboard – right
th' - the
thar - there
ye - you
yerself - yourself
youse – you are

PIRATE LINGO

- **Arrrr** – add to every sentence you say for pirate emphasis
- **Shiver me timbers** – say whenever surprised and shout it as loud as you can
- **Everythin' shipshape** – make sure everything is tidy and in orde
- **Yo, ho, ho** – this is how you should laugh
- **Dash my buttons** – have a laugh
- **All hands on deck** – all monsters should be on the ship's deck
- **Land ho** – land in sight
- **Land lubbers** – monsters who stay on land
- **Sea dog** – a monster pirate who has been at sea for some time
- **Walk the plank** – just do as it says!

Find out about Cap'n Buck's latest pirate adventures by reading this message we found in a mouldy old bottle on the shores of the Port. Can you guess where he is?

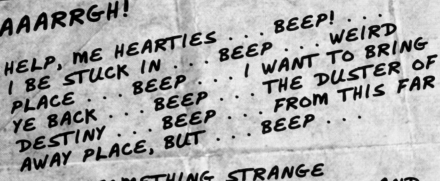

CAP'N BUCK IS AT

....

AAARRGH!

HELP, ME HEARTIES . . . BEEP!
I BE STUCK IN . . . BEEP . . . BEEP! . . .
PLACE . . . BEEP . . . I WANT TO BRING
YE BACK . . . BEEP . . . THE DUSTER OF
DESTINY . . . BEEP . . . FROM THIS FAR
AWAY PLACE, BUT . . . BEEP . . .

SOMETHING STRANGE
HAPPENED . . . BEEP . . . AND
I BE IN ANOTHER . . . BEEP . . .
DIMENSION . . . BEEP!

I FEEL . . . BEEP . . . TRANSPORTED
. . . BEEP . . . THROUGH TIME . . . BEEP
. . . AND SPACE . . . BEEP . . . INTO . . .
RUSHIN' . . . BEEP . . . WATER . . . BEEP
. . . FALLS . . . IN THE . . . BEEP . . .
BACK TO THE . . . BEEP

IT BE VERY VAST . . . BEEP . . . AND THE
OPPOSITE OF . . . BEEP . . . TH' . . . PAST

I BE SURROUNDED BY . . . BEEP . . .
ROBOT BUTLERS . . . BEEP . . . AND . . .
TECHNOLOGY . . . BEEP . . . TAKING OVER
. . . BEEP

CAN YE LOOK INTO YER . . . BEEP
MYSTIC . . . BEEP . . . 9 BALL TO
FIND OUT WHERE I . . . BEEP . . . ?
OR MAY . . . BEEP . . . AGONY ANT
BEEP . . . COULD HELP YE . . .?

BE QUICK. . . OR I MAY . . . BEEP. . .
STUCK HERE. . . BEEP. . . FOREVER.

BUCK

45

SHIPMATE!

Being a pirate involves tactical manoeuvres, as you navigate your way through the sometimes treacherous waves of Potion Ocean. Find a shipmate and play this game to prepare yerself for a pioneering pirate's life at sea.

WHAT TO DO:

1. When you have finished reading this book, pull out or photocopy the opposite page and give two grids, A and B, and a pencil to each player.

2. Each player has a grid for their own ships, A, and a grid to track where the other player's ships are, B. On grid A, draw where your ships are, as shown. You have five different 'ships' to add and they are all different sizes. (See Ship Size grid at bottom of next page.)

3. Make sure your opponent doesn't see where you have placed your ships.
Take it in turns to guess the coordinates of the other player's ships. When the other player guesses a square where part of one of your ships is, shout 'hit'. When they guess a square where you have no ships, shout 'miss!', in your loudest piratey voice.

4. Mark an X on grid B when you guess correctly where part of the other player's ships are. Mark an O on grid B when you find out their ship isn't there.

5. The winner is the player to sink all the other player's ships first, and shout out 'shipmate!'

A.

	A	B	C	D	E	F	G	H	I	J
1										
2										
3										
4										
5										
6										
7										
8										
9										
0										

	A	B	C	D	E	F	G	H	I	J
1										
2										
3										
4										
5										
6										
7										
8										
9										
10										

	A	B	C	D	E	F	G	H	I	J
1										
2										
3										
4										
5										
6										
7										
8										
9										
10										

	A	B	C	D	E	F	G	H	I	J
1										
2										
3										
4										
5										
6										
7										
8										
9										
10										

A.

B.

SHIP SIZES

Cloudy Cloth Clipper = 5 squares long
Gift Island Ferry = 4 squares long
Old Fishing Boat = 3 squares long
Life Boat = 3 squares long
Lenny Lard's Rubber Ring = 2 squares long

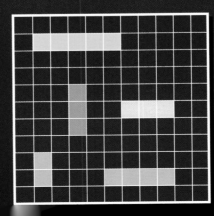

Switchy Day!

8th OCTOBER

Congratulations to nay76767, the monSTAR creator of Monstro City's fabulously funny new celebration – Switchy Day! This is the day when everything will be switchified. Monsters have to dress up just like their owners, owners can dress up like their monsters and everyone can walk, talk, eat and sleep the wrong way around. So buy a Backwards Puzzle Clock, get your mind crazily confused, and be ready for the switching hour, full of bamboozling itchy-switchy business. You'll be struggling to see switch monster is switch from bedtime, to lunch, to breakfast!

Things to do on Switchy Day

First, all monsters should **walk backwards** to The Marketplace and rummage through the human-face items on sale. Does your owner have a three-foot long moustache? If so, you'd better be switching to wear it, even if it feels painfully switchy.

Owners should race the wrong way to the Print Workshop on Ooh La Lane and **make a monster mask** to wear. It'll be like you and your owner just switched places – spooky!

Buy some Un-Smiley Flowers for your room just for Switchy Day. How can you help but frown with these flowers turned upside down? Found frowning at a Bazaar Bizarre near you, only on Switchy Day.

Chomp on a delicious **Upside-Down Fairy Cake** from the Gross-ery Store – eat it before it flies away, upside down and backwards!

Paste up some topsy-turvy Upside Down Stormy Wallpaper from Yukea, and watch it rain back into the sky – at least you won't get wet!

Bizarre Bazaar's Bobbing Balloons bob upside down and **float on the floor** instead of the ceiling, so catch some and take them home.

To claim your exclusive Switchy Day virtual gift, go to the sign-in page of

MOSHIMONSTERS.COM

and enter the name of the monster who created Switchy Day!

TORCHLIGHT TALES

31st OCTOBER

What does October bring? Halloween, of course! So dress yourself up in your scariest costumes, read these spooky tale tips, grab a torch, turn out the lights and tell some spooky stories to your Moshi friends. Try not to scare yourself Silly Chilli! Mwa, ha, ha, ha!

SCARY FAIRY-TAIL TIPS

• Start by creating the **right atmosphere.** If you live in a Haunted House, then perfect. If not, decorate your room with the Bat Mobile, Bats Wallpaper, some Wall Bats and hang up a Spider Chandelier.

• Dress up like Fronkenshteen (Neck Bolts compulsory), a vampire with the Vamp's Cloak and Fangs, a Weremon (Gloves, Mask, Shirt and Shoes are available), or a Wicked Witch (Broom, dress, hat, hair and nose can all be bought).

• When your listeners arrive, serve Bug Juice, Crispy Bat Wings and Eye Pie. Or how about Pumpkin Chowder and Spider Lollies for any younger guests with sweet fangs?

• Come up with a **scary name** for your story and **set the scene.** If you make your story seem like it could be happening right now, that will make it even more scary!

• **Scary characters** you could use are the bloodsucking Furry Heebees, Baby Ghosts, Dr. Strangeglove, Weremen, Fronkenshteen or even Simon Growl! You can also make up your very own mystery scary Moshi Monster.

• Begin by speaking slowly and softly, and then when something really scary happens shout it out exscreamly **LOUD!!!** That's bound to make everyone jump!

• Try to add in phrases like 'she's come to get us' and screams like 'eeeeeeeeeeeeeeeeeeeeeeek'!

• All torchlight tales are best told using scary **sound effects and props** wherever possible. For example, if you want to do scary footstep sounds, stomp around the room.

• Add lots of **scary laughing** in wherever possible, mwah, ha, ha, ha! For example if you say 'forever', change it to FOREVA, HA, HA, HA!

• Great scary words you can add to your story include: boo, bat, witch, web, shake, screech, howling, growling, swoop, chilling, bang, sickly, stomp, skeleton, moon, broom, fly, cackle, scare, haunted, ghost, gobbling, sneak, brew, cauldron, rattling, bones.

Wishing you a fangtastic Halloween storytelling time!

Tamara Tesla's Extreme Teasers

Do you have what it takes to try out these super, tricky challenges? Are you an egghead, or will your brain be scrambled or fried like an egg forever? Try these puzzles out to see.

Give yourself sixty seconds and see how many you can get right in the time.

SCARE SQUARES

How many squares are there in each of these four boxes?

 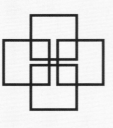  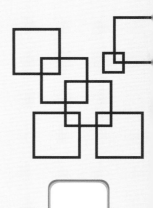

NEXT NUMBER

What numbers come next in these sequences?

2, 6, 18, 36, 72, ____

5, 8, 11, 14, 17, ____

79, 70, 61, 52, ____

BUBBLE TROUBLE

Which coloured bubble is not touching the black bubbles?

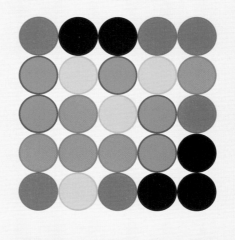

JIGSAW JAM

Which coloured jigsaw piece matches the white one in the middle?

LINE DANCE

Which line is the longest?

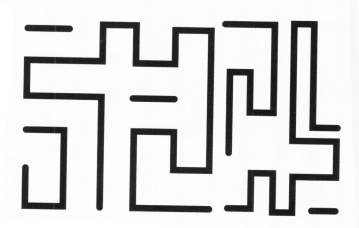

CHOCK A BLOCK

How many blocks are in this shape?

INVENTIONS

Tamara loves conjuring up puzzles, but she also enjoys creating crazy inventions. She particularly likes her Fry-While-You're-Flying Machine, in which the name says it all. Unfortunately, she is still trying to get that particular idea off the ground. Use this section of Tamara's Smart Mind = Smart Monsters notebook to make up your very own invention.

Giving Thanks

24th NOVEMBER

Here are Monstro City's top ten things to give fangks for on Thanksgiving day this year . . .

1. Cap'n Buck bringing us back such bootiful booty from beyond

2. Tyra Fangs and all her fanciful gossip and fabulous fashion advice

3. Roary Scrawl's journalistic genius

4. All you Super Moshis out there – you know who you are and Monstro City shall always need your help

5. Buster Bumblechops for all our lovely furry Moshling friends and his extraordinary tracking tips

6. Starlight Cookies – because they fell to earth and they're yummola

7. Furry Luv Chairs – we LUV, LUV, LUV them and without LUV what is there? LUV makes the world go round (so fast it makes us sick!)

8. Simon Growl, for his brutal honesty and judging of us

9. Roy G Biv bringing colour to our lives, time and time again (well, on Roy G Biv day at least.)

10. Moshi madness – yes, every Moshi adds to the monSTARness that is Monstro City, and we thank each and every single Moshi-mad one of you!

What would you like to give thanks for

Write a list here:

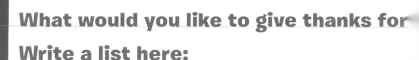

THANK YOU FOR THE MUSIC

This time of year is perfect for making up your very own festive monster-raving playlist. Will you choose Flop Pop, Green-eared Soul, Indie Roxs, Forkronica, Tech-yes, Grime or all that dances between? With so much mu-sick choice you may need a little hand, so try out the top eleven tunes below that we feel you should be fan-full for.

NOTE: We tried to do a top ten countdown, but had eleven favourite tunes.

11  Old in at number 11: **Hairosniff** with *Poppet (Looks like a Furi)*

10  Climbing, rather than falling, to number 10: **Banana Montana** with *The Fall*

9  Slipping on its buttery side down to number 9: Taylor **Miffed** (we think she might be a bit miffed) with *Bred to Toast*

8  Groaning and moaning all the way to number 8, it's the **Groanas Brothers** with *Growliwood*

7  Running ahead to number 7, it's **The Goo Fighters** and *Forget to Walk*

6  Being followed all the way to number 6, it's her Ladyship **Lady Googoo** with *Peppy-razzi*

5  Archering a spot at number 5 is **Broccoli Spears** with her *Peppermizer*

4  Keeping the cost down at number 4 is **49 Pence** and *Catch a Pitch or Try Cryin'*

3  Hot on their furry tails at number 3, it's the **Pussycat Poppets** and *Pipe Down*

2  Not quite ready to fizzy pop their way to the number one spot, at number 2 it's **The Fizzbangs** with *Monstrocity*

1 And greeting number one and the top of the charts with a happy clappy tune to blow our minds, it's *Hey Moshi* – sung by all the biggest Moshi fans. Go on, join in, you know you want to!

THE ROAD TO MONSTAR-DOM

It can be a long Sludgey Street for some and a short hop, skip and jump along Ooh La Lane for others, but the road to monSTAR-dom is full of lumps, bumps and fascinating stories. Read on to find out how some of Monstro City's famous fiends got where they are today.

Broccoli Spears

Oops . . . she did it again! Yes folks, Broccoli Spears is the pot-bound veggie vocalist who's constantly baffling fans with her *ahem* **strange behaviour.** Starting as a sweet innocent stem, she then shocked the world by chopping off her florets and appearing at an in-store signing dressed as a cauliflower! According to her manager, she was 'exhausted' following a night out with her popstar pal Celery Gruff, but critics think she could be **heading for another meltdown** – and that's bad news because miming along to smash hits like *Boil Me Baby One More Time* and *Fertilizer* isn't easy when you're a soggy mess.

LADY GOO GOO

Some say she's crazy, some say she's a genius. One thing's for sure, the Moshi world has gone completely **gaga for Lady Goo Goo!** But it's not down to her plinkity plink music (although *Coochie Coo* and *Peppy-razzi* are real toe-tappers) or even her baby-ish dance routines. It's because this wah-wah-ing bundle of joy is a **fashion icon!** Goo Goo came onto the music scene wearing gleaming Rox-covered romper suits and riding in a futuristic tinfoil pram. She was hard to miss, especially if she started boohoo-ing when she didn't get her way. She's not really a cry baby, it's just that she must have her milky-wilk on the hour, every hour. With her whole grown-up life ahead of her, it looks like she's here to stay for quite some crying times.

GOO FIGHTERS

This fearsome four-piece got together during the grunge period and never looked back. Lead singer Davy Gravy was once a member of legendary band **Blurgh-varna**, but decided to form a new outfit following a (really sticky) jam session with Squint Beastford, the Goo's one-eyed drummer, down at the Slimelite nightclub. Often compared to old-school grunge act, Hurl Jam, the Goo Fighters are always touring and recently packed out the Firebowl Stadium. Davy's even made a **guest appearance** on the Moshi movie, *School of Drool*. Things have never looked gooey-er!

Groanas Brothers

Squeaky clean and perfect in every way, the Groanas Brothers are so wholesome it hurts. That's why their **success is baffling,** because here in Monstro City music fans like their stars to be gooey, ucky, weird and monstery. Seen as the ultimate alternative band, this **handsome trio** started out as guests on Banana Montana's *MonstroVision* show before supporting (and blowing away) ancient boy band N-Stink. Now bigger than ever, the Groanas Brothers are busy starring in their **own reality show**, where fans can see them fixing their hair, standing around with their hands in their pockets and changing their outfits every five minutes.

THE TWELVE DAYS OF TWISTMAS

On the first day of Twistmas,
Buster Bumblechops gave to me . . .
A party in Monstro City!

On the second day of Twistmas,
Buster Bumblechops gave to me . . .
Two tasty Turkoys,
And a party in Monstro City!

On the third day of Twistmas,
Buster Bumblechops gave to me . . .
Three Silly Chillies,
Two tasty Turkoys,
And a party in Monstro City!

On the fourth day of Twistmas,
Buster Bumblechops gave to me . . .
Four fluffy Moshlings,
Three Silly Chillies,
Two tasty Turkoys,
And a party in
Monstro City!

Get into the spirit of Twistmas and sing along with the Moshi Twistmas scare-rollers!

On the fifth day of Twistmas,
Buster Bumblechops gave to me . . .
Five . . . Fried Egg . . . Rugs . . .
Four fluffy Moshlings,
Three Silly Chillies,
Two tasty Turkoys,
And a party in Monstro City!

On the sixth day of Twistmas,
Buster Bumblechops gave to me . . .
Six seeds a-growing,
Five . . . Fried Egg . . . Rugs . . .
Four fluffy Moshlings,
Three Silly Chillies,
Two tasty Turkoys,
And a party in Monstro City!

On the seventh day of Twistmas,
Buster Bumblechops gave to me . . .
Seven 'Sumas swimming,
Six seeds a-growing,
Five . . . Fried Egg . . . Rugs . . .
Four fluffy Moshlings,
Three Silly Chillies,
Two tasty Turkoys,
And a party in Monstro City!

On the eighth day of Twistmas,
Buster Bumblechops gave to me . . .
Eight Diavlos dancing,
Seven 'Sumas swimming,
Six seeds a-growing,
Five . . . Fried Egg . . . Rugs . . .
Four fluffy Moshlings,
Three Silly Chillies,
Two tasty Turkoys,
And a party in Monstro City!

On the ninth day of Twistmas,
Buster Bumblechops gave to me . . .
Nine Poppets prancing,
Eight Diavlos dancing,
Seven 'Sumas swimming,
Six seeds a-growing,
Five . . . Fried Egg . . . Rugs . . .
Four fluffy Moshlings,
Three Silly Chillies,
Two tasty Turkoys,
And a party in Monstro City!

On the tenth day of Twistmas,
Buster Bumblechops gave to me . . .
Ten Furis frowning,
Nine Poppets prancing,
Eight Diavlos dancing,
Seven 'Sumas swimming,
Six seeds a-growing,
Five . . . Fried Egg . . . Rugs . . .
Four fluffy Moshlings,
Three Silly Chillies,
Two tasty Turkoys,
And a party in Monstro City!

**On the eleventh day of Twistmas,
Buster Bumblechops gave to me . . .**
Eleven Luvlis lying,
Ten Furis frowning,
Nine Poppets prancing,
Eight Diavlos dancing,
Seven 'Sumas swimming,
Six seeds a-growing,
Five . . . Fried Egg . . . Rugs . . .
Four fluffy Moshlings,
Three Silly Chillies,
Two tasty Turkoys,
And a party in Monstro City!

**On the twelfth day of Twistmas,
Buster Bumblechops gave to me . . .**
Twelve Zommers zinging,
Eleven Luvlis lying,
Ten Furis frowning,
Nine Poppets prancing,
Eight Diavlos dancing,
Seven 'Sumas swimming,
Six seeds a-growing,
Five . . . Fried Egg . . . Rugs . . .
Four furry Moshlings,
Three Silly Chillies,
Two tasty Turkoys,
And a par. . . ty . . . in . . .
Mon. . . stro Ci. . .ty!

Snow Joke

When you've decorated your room with Snowy Wallpaper, Snowy Floor, Snowy Windows and Snowy Door, invite everyone around to your snow-place-like-home winter wonderland, and try out some of these snowy classics. Everyone will be rolling around singing *Freeze a Jolly Good Fellow* to you in snow time at all!

What do you get when you cross a snowman and a vampire?

Frostbite!

What do you call a very old snowman?

Water!

What do you get when you cross Frosty with a baker?

Frosty the Dough-man!

What does the ferocious abominable snowman eat for breakfast?

Snowflakes!

Who gives presents to children and bites them too?

Santa Jaws!

How do snowmen travel around?

By icecycle.

Who is the most famous Twistmas elf?

Elfvis

Knock, knock
Who's there?
Snow
Snow who?
Snow use, I've forgotten my name!

Where does a snowma keep his money?

In a snow bank!

The End of the Year Round-up

So, it's that time of year when we like to take a look back at what a fab time we've had! Take a look back at page eight – did you keep your resolutions? What were your top monster moments?

I kept _____ of my resolutions and failed to keep _____ of them!

The top three things I would like to do next year are:
1.
2.
3.

My award for MonSTAR of the year goes to: _____

My award for MonSTAR room of the year goes to: _____

My Maddest Monster Moment was: _____

I wish you could _____ on Moshi Monsters!

ROARY SCRAWL

Check out *The Daily Growl* for all the ooze that's fit to print and comment on the stories and competitions to win great prizes!

Activity Answers

Page 4
There are 54 of Dr. Strangeglove's Glumps hidden in this book.

Page 19
Interview with a Monster
Cap'n Buck's treasure is Sunglasses.

Page 28
How Does your Moshling Garden Grow. . .?

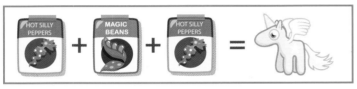

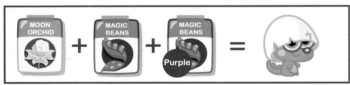

Page 45
Message in a Bottle
Cap'n Buck is at Futuristic Falls.

Pages 50-51
Tamara Tesla's Challenges

Scare Squares
7, 8, 12, 12

Next Number
144, 20, 43

Bubble Trouble
Green

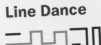

Jigsaw Jam
Green

Line Dance

Chock a Block
6, 12, 43

ALSO AVAILABLE:

ISBN: 978-1409390350
THE MOSHLING COLLECTOR'S GUIDE
With exclusive secret Moshling!

ISBN: 978-1409390435
MONSTAR ROOMS HANDBOOK
WITH LOADS OF STICKERS AND FREE COOL DOWNLOAD FOR YOUR ROOM!

ISBN: 9781409390442

FANGTASTIC ACTIVITY BOOK
OVER 40 STICKERS

ISBN: 978-1409390541

BUSTER'S LOST MOSHLINGS: A Search-and-Find Book

ISBN: 978-1409390527
GAME ON!
Tips, Tricks and Cheats
For over 40 Moshi Mini Games
Includes exclusive virtual gift for your room!

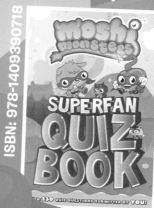
ISBN: 978-1409390718
SUPERFAN QUIZ BOOK
OVER 230 QUIZ QUESTIONS SUBMITTED BY YOU!

ISBN: 978-1409390459
MY MOSHI MONSTERS JOKE BOOK
HA! HA! HA! HA!
WITH OVER 230 MONSTER-TICKLING JOKES SUBMITTED BY YOU!